Tertullian
The Apology

Tertullian
The Apology

Tertullian
The Apology

© Lighthouse Publishing 2015

All rights reserved. Without limiting the rights under copyright reserved above, no part of this publication may be reproduced, stored in a retrieval system, or transmitted, in any form or by any means (electronic, mechanical, photocopying, recording or otherwise), without the prior written permission of the copyright owner of this book.

Published by
Lighthouse Christian Publishing
SAN 257-4330
5531 Dufferin Drive
Savage, Minnesota, 55378
United States of America

www.lighthousechristianpublishing.com

Tertullian

Introductory Note.

[a.d. 145–220.] When our Lord repulsed the woman of Canaan (Matt. xv. 22) with apparent harshness, he applied to her people the epithet *dogs*, with which the children of Israel had thought it piety to reproach them. When He accepted her faith and caused it to be recorded for our learning, He did something more: He reversed the curse of the Canaanite and showed that the Church was designed "for all people;" Catholic alike for all time and for all sorts and conditions of men.

Thus the North-African Church was loved before it was born: the Good Shepherd was gently leading those "that were with young." Here was the charter of those Christians to be a Church, who then were Canaanites in the land of their father Ham. It is remarkable indeed that among these pilgrims and strangers to the West the first elements of Latin Christianity come into view. Even at the close of the Second Century the Church in Rome is an inconsiderable, though prominent, member of the great confederation of Christian Churches which has its chief seats in Alexandria and Antioch, and of which the entire Literature is Greek. It is an African presbyter who takes from Latin Christendom the reproach of theological and literary barrenness and begins the great work in which, upon his foundations, Cyprian and Augustine built up, with incomparable genius, that Carthaginian School of Christian thought by which Latin Theology was dominated for centuries. It is important to note (1.) that providentially not one of these illustrious doctors died in Communion with the Roman See, pure though it was and venerable at that time; and (2.) that to the works of Augustine the Reformation in Germany and Continental Europe was largely due; while (3.) the *specialties* of the Anglican Reformation were, in like proportion, due to the writings of Tertullian and Cyprian. The hinges of great and controlling destinies for Western Europe and our own America are to be found in the period we are now approaching.

The merest school-boy knows much of the history of Carthage, and how the North Africans became Roman citizens. How they became Christians is not so clear. A melancholy destiny has enveloped Carthage from the outset, and its glory and greatness as a Christian See were transient indeed. It blazed out all at once in Tertullian, after about a century of missionary labors had been exerted upon its creation: and having given a Minucius Felix, an Arnobius and a Lactantius to adorn the earliest period of Western Ecclesiastical learning, in addition to its nobler luminaries, it rapidly declined. At the beginning of the Third Century, at a council presided over by Agrippinus, Bishop of Carthage, there were present not less than seventy bishops of the Province. A period of cruel persecutions followed, and the African Church received a baptism of blood.

Tertullian was born a heathen, and seems to have been educated at Rome, where he probably practiced as a jurisconsult. We may, perhaps, adopt most of the ideas of Allix, as conjecturally probable, and assign his birth to a.d. 145. He became a Christian about 185, and a presbyter about 190. The period of his strict orthodoxy very nearly expires with the century. He lived to an extreme old age, and some suppose even till a.d. 240. More probably we must adopt the date preferred by recent writers, a.d. 220.

It seems to be the fashion to treat of Tertullian as a Montanist, and only incidentally to celebrate his services to the Catholic Orthodoxy of Western Christendom. Were I his biographer I should reverse this course, as a mere act of justice, to say nothing of gratitude to a man of splendid intellect, to whom the filial spirit of Cyprian accorded the loving tribute of a disciple, and whose genius stamped itself upon the very words of Latin theology, and prepared the language for the labors of a Jerome. In creating the Vulgate, and so lifting the Western Churches into a position of intellectual equality with the East, the latter as well as St. Augustine himself were debtors to Tertullian in a degree not to be estimated by any other than the Providential Mind that inspired his brilliant career as a Christian.

In speaking of Tatian I laid the base for what I wished to say of Tertullian. Let God only be their judge; let us gratefully recognize the debt we owe to them. Let us read them, as we read the works of King Solomon. We must, indeed, approve of the discipline of the Primitive Age, which allowed of no compromises. The Church was struggling for existence, and could not permit any man to become her master. The more brilliant the intellect, the more dangerous to the poor Church were its perversions of her Testimony. Before the heathen tribunals, and in the market-places, it would not answer to let Christianity appear double tongued. The orthodoxy of the Church, not less than her children, was undergoing an ordeal of fire. It seems a miracle that her Testimony preserved its unity, and that heresy was branded as such by the instinct of the Faithful. Poor Tertullian was cut off by his own act. The weeping Church might bewail him as David mourned for Absalom, but like David, she could not give the Ark of God into other hands than those of the loyal and the true. I have set the writings of Tertullian in a natural and logical order, so as to aid the student, and to relieve him from the distractions of such an arrangement as one finds in Oehler's edition. Valuable as it is, the practical use of it is irritating and confusing. The reader

of that edition may turn to the slightly differing schemes of
Neander and Kaye, for a theoretical order of the works; but
here he will find a classification which will aid his inquiries.
He will find, first, those works which connect with the
Apologists of the former volumes of this series: which illustrate
the Church's position toward the outside world, the Jews as
well as the Gentiles. Next come those works which contend
with internal differences and heresies. And then, those which
reflect the morals and manners of Christians. These are classed
with some reference to their degrees of freedom from the
Montanistic taint, and are followed, last of all, by the few tracts
which belong to the melancholy period of his lapse, and are
directed against the Church's orthodoxy.

  Let it be borne in mind, that if this sad close of
Tertullian's career cannot be extenuated, the later history of
Latin Christianity forbids us to condemn him, in the tones
which proceeded from the Virgin Church with authority, and
which the law of her testimony and the instinct of self-
preservation forced her to utter. Let us reflect that St. Bernard
and after him the Schoolmen, whom we so deservedly honor,
separated themselves far more absolutely than ever Tertullian
did from the orthodoxy of Primitive Christendom. The schism
which withdrew the West from Communion with the original
seats of Christendom, and from Nicene Catholicity, was
formidable beyond all expression, in comparison with
Tertullian's entanglements with a delusion which the See of
Rome itself had momentarily patronized. Since the Council of
Trent, not a theologian of the Latins has been free from organic
heresies, compared with which the fanaticism of our author
was a trifling aberration. Since the late Council of the Vatican,
essential Montanism has become organized in the Latin
Churches: for what are the new revelations and oracles of the
pontiff but the *deliria* of another claimant to the voice and
inspiration of the Paraclete? Poor Tertullian! The sad
influences of his decline and folly have been fatally felt in all
the subsequent history of the West, but, surely subscribers to

the Modern Creed of the Vatican have reason to "speak gently of *their father's* fall." To Döllinger, with the "Old Catholic" remnant only, is left the right to name the Montanists heretics, or to upbraid Tertullian as a lapser from Catholicity.

From Dr. Holmes, I append the following Introductory Notice:

(I.) Quintus Septimius Florens Tertullianus, as our author is called in the mss. of his works, is thus noticed by Jerome in his *Catalogus Scriptorum Ecclesiasticorum:* "Tertullian, a presbyter, the first Latin writer after Victor and Apollonius, was a native of the province of Africa and city of Carthage, the son of a proconsular centurion: he was a man of a sharp and vehement temper, flourished under Severus and Antoninus Caracalla, and wrote numerous works, which (as they are generally known) I think it unnecessary to particularize. I saw at Concordia, in Italy, an old man named Paulus. He said that when young he had met at Rome with an aged amanuensis of the blessed Cyprian, who told him that Cyprian never passed a day without reading some portion of Tertullian's works, and used frequently to say, *Give me my master*, meaning Tertullian. After remaining a presbyter of the church until he had attained the middle age of life, Tertullian was, by the envy and contumelious treatment of the Roman clergy, driven to embrace the opinions of Montanus, which he has mentioned in several of his works under the title of the New Prophecy....He is reported to have lived to a very advanced age, and to have composed many other works which are not extant." We add Bishop Kaye's notes on this extract, in an abridged shape: "The correctness of some parts of this account has been questioned. Doubts have been entertained whether Tertullian was a presbyter, although these have solely arisen from Roman Catholic objections to a married priesthood; for it is certain that he was married, there being among his works two treatises addressed to his wife....Another question has been raised respecting the place where Tertullian officiated as a presbyter—whether at Carthage or at Rome. That he at one time resided at Carthage may be inferred from Jerome's statement, and is rendered certain by several passages of his own writings. Allix supposes that the notion of his having been a presbyter of the Roman Church owed its rise to what Jerome said of the envy and abuse of the Roman clergy impelling him to espouse the party of Montanus. Optatus, and the author of the work *de Hæresibus*, which Sirmond edited under the title of Prædestinatus, expressly call him a Carthaginian presbyter. Semler, however, in a dissertation inserted in his edition of Tertullian's works, contends that he was a presbyter of the Roman Church. Eusebius tells us that he was accurately acquainted with the Roman laws, and on other accounts a distinguished person at Rome. Tertullian displays, moreover, a knowledge of the proceedings of the Roman Church with respect to Marcion and Valentinus, who were once members of it, which could scarcely have been obtained by one who had not himself been numbered amongst its presbyters Semler admits that, after Tertullian seceded from the church, he left and returned to Carthage. Jerome does not inform us whether Tertullian was born of Christian parents, or was converted to Christianity. There are passages in his writings which seem to imply that he had been a Gentile; yet he may perhaps mean to describe, not his own condition, but that of Gentiles in general, before their conversion. Allix and the majority of commentators understand them literally, as well as some other passages in which he speaks of his own infirmities and sinfulness. His writings show that he flourished at the period specified by Jerome—that is, during the reigns of Severus and Antoninus Caracalla, or between the years a.d. 193 and 216; but they supply no precise information respecting the date of his birth, or any of the principal occurrences of his life. Allix places his birth about 145 or 150; his conversion to Christianity about a.d. 185; his marriage about 186; his admission to the priesthood about 192; his adoption of the opinions of Montanus about 199; and his death about a.d. 220.

But these dates, it must be understood, rest entirely on conjecture."

(II.) Tertullian's work against Marcion, as it happens, is, *as to its date*, the best authenticated—perhaps the only well authenticated—particular connected with the author's life. He himself mentions the fifteenth year of the reign of Severus as the time when he was writing the work: "Ad xv. jam Severi imperatoris." This agrees with Jerome's Chronicle, where occurs this note: "Anno 2223 Severi xv° Tertullianus...celebratur." This year is assigned to the year of our Lord 207; but notwithstanding the certainty of this date, it is far from clear that it describes more than the time of the publication of *the first book*. On the contrary, it is nearly certain that the other books, although connected manifestly enough in the author's argument and purpose (compare the initial and the final chapters of the several books), were yet issued at separate times. Noesselt shows that between the Book i. and Books ii.–iv. Tertullian issued his *De Præscript. Hæret.*, and previous to Book v. he published his tracts, *De Carne Christi* and *De Resurrectione Carnis*. After giving the incontestable date of the xv. of Severus for the first book, he says it is a mistake to suppose that the other books were published with it. He adds: "Although we cannot undertake to determine whether Tertullian issued his Books ii., iii., iv., against Marcion, together or separately, or in what year, we yet venture to affirm that Book v. appeared apart from the rest. For the tract *De Resurr. Carnis* appears from its second chapter to have been published after the tract *De Carne Christi*, in which latter work (chap. vii.) he quotes a passage from the fourth book against Marcion. But in his Book v. against Marcion (chap. x.), he refers to his work *De Resurr. Carnis*; which circumstance makes it evident that Tertullian published his Book v. at a different time from his Book iv. In his Book i. he announces his intention (chap. i.) of some time or other completing his tract *De Præscript. Hæret.*, but in his book *De Carne Christi* (chap. ii.), he mentions how he had completed it,—a conclusive proof that his Book i. against Marcion preceded the other books."

(III.) Respecting Marcion himself, the most formidable heretic who had as yet opposed revealed truth, enough will turn up in this treatise, with the notes which we have added in explanation, to satisfy the reader. It will, however, be convenient to give here a few introductory particulars of him. Tertullian mentions Marcion as being, with Valentinus, in communion with the Church at Rome, "under the episcopate of the blessed Eleutherus." He goes on to charge them with "ever-restless curiosity, with which they infected even the brethren;" and informs us that they were more than once put out of communion—"Marcion, indeed, with the 200 sesterces which he brought into the church." He goes on to say, that "being at last condemned to the banishment of a perpetual separation, they sowed abroad the poisons of their doctrines. Afterwards, when Marcion, having professed penitence, agreed to the terms offered to him, that he should receive reconciliation on condition that he brought back to the church the rest also, whom he had trained up for perdition, he was prevented by death." He was a native of Sinope in Pontus, of which city, according to an account preserved by Epiphanius, which, however, is somewhat doubtful, his father was bishop, and of high character both for his orthodoxy and exemplary practice. He came to Rome soon after the death of Hyginus, probably about a.d. 141 or 142; and soon after his arrival he adopted the heresy of Cerdon.

(IV.) It is an interesting question as to what edition of the Holy Scriptures Tertullian used in his very copious quotations. It may at once be asserted that he did not cite from the Hebrew, although some writers have claimed for him, among his varied learning, a knowledge of the sacred language. Bp. Kaye observes, page 61, n. 1, that "he sometimes speaks as if he was acquainted with Hebrew," and refers to the *Anti-Marcion* iv. 39, the *Adv. Praxeam* v., and the *Adv. Judæos* ix. Be this as it may, it is manifest that Tertullian's Scripture passages never resemble the Hebrew, but in nearly every instance the Septuagint, whenever, as is most frequently the case, that version differs from the original. In the New Testament there is, as might be expected, a tolerably close conformity to the Greek. There is, however, it must be allowed, a sufficiently frequent variation from the letter of both the Greek Testaments to justify Semler's suspicion that Tertullian always quoted from the old Latin version, whatever that might have been, which was current in the African church in the second and third centuries. The most valuable part of Semler's *Dissertatio de varia et incerta indole Librorum Q. S. F. Tertulliani* is his investigation of this very point. In section iv. he endeavors to prove this proposition: "Hic scriptor non in manibus habuit Græcos libros sacros;" and he states his conclusion thus: "Certissimum est nec Tertullianum nec Cyprianum nec ullum scriptorem e Latinis illis ecclesiasticis provocare unquam ad Græcorum librorum auctoritatem si vel maxime obscura aut contraria lectio occurreret;" and again: "Ex his satis certum est, Latinos satis diu secutos fuisse auctoritatem suorum librorum adversus Græcos, nec concessisse nisi serius, cum Augustini et Hieronymi nova auctoritas juvare videretur." It is not ignorance of Greek which is imputed to Tertullian, for he is said to have well understood that language, and even to have composed in it. He probably followed the Latin, as writers now usually quote the authorized English, as being current and best known among their readers. Independent feeling, also, would have weight with such a temper as Tertullian's, to say nothing of the suspicion which largely prevailed in the African branch of the Latin church, that the Greek copies of the Scriptures were much corrupted by the heretics, who were chiefly, if not wholly, Greeks or Greek-speaking persons.

(V.) Whatever perverting effect Tertullian's secession to the sect of Montanus may have had on his judgment in his latest writings, it did not vitiate the work against Marcion. With a few trivial exceptions, this treatise may be read by the

The Apology

strictest Catholic without any feeling of annoyance. His lapse to Montanism is set down conjecturally as having taken place a.d. 199. Jerome, we have seen, attributed the event to his quarrel with the Roman clergy, but this is at least doubtful; nor must it be forgotten that Tertullian's mind seems to have been peculiarly suited by nature to adopt the mystical notions and ascetic principles of Montanus. It is satisfactory to find that, on the whole, "the authority of Tertullian," as the learned Dr. Burton says, "upon great points of doctrine is considered to be little, if at all, affected by his becoming a Montanist." (*Lectures on Eccl. Hist.* vol. ii. p. 234.) Besides the different works which are expressly mentioned in the notes of this volume, recourse has been had by the translator to Dupin's *Hist. Eccl. Writers* (trans.), vol. i. pp. 69–86; Tillemont's *Mèmoires Hist. Eccl.* iii. 85–103; Dr. Smith's *Greek and Roman Biography*, articles "Marcion" and "Tertullian;" Schaff's article, in Herzog's *Cyclopædia*, on "Tertullian;" Munter's *Primordia Eccl. Africanæ*, pp. 118–150; Robertson's *Church Hist.* vol. i. pp. 70–77; Dr. P. Schaff's *Hist. of Christian Church* (New York, 1859, pp. 511–519), and Archdeacon Evans' *Biography of the Early Church*, vol. i. (Lives of "Marcion," pp. 93–122, and "Tertullian," pp. 325–363). This last work, though of a popular cast, shows a good deal of research and learning, expressed in the pleasant style of the once popular author of *The Rectory of Vale Head*. The translator has mentioned these works, because they are all quite accessible to the general reader, and will give him adequate information concerning the subject treated in the present volume.

    To this introduction of Dr. Holmes must be added that of Mr. Thelwall, the translator of the Third volume in the Edinburgh Series, as follows:

    To arrange chronologically the works (especially if numerous) of an author whose own date is known with tolerable precision, is not always or necessarily easy: witness the controversies as to the succession of St. Paul's epistles. To do this in the case of an author whose own date is itself a matter of controversy may therefore be reasonably expected to be still less so; and such is the predicament of him who attempts to perform this task for Tertullian. I propose to give a specimen or two of the difficulties with which the task is beset; and then to lay before the reader briefly a summary of the results at which eminent scholars, who have devoted much time and thought to the subject, have arrived. Such a course, I think, will at once afford him means of judging of the absolute impossibility of arriving at definite certainty in the matter; and induce him to excuse me if I prefer furnishing him with materials from which to deduce his own conclusions, rather than venturing on an *ex cathedra* decision on so doubtful a subject.

I. The book, as Dr. Holmes has reminded us, of the date of which we seem to have the surest evidence, is *Adv. Marc.* i. This book was in course of writing, as its author himself (c. 15) tells us, "in the fifteenth year of the empire of Severus." Now this date would be clear if there were no doubt as to which year of our era corresponds to Tertullian's fifteenth of Severus. Pamelius, however, says Dr. Holmes, makes it a.d. 208; Clinton, (whose authority is more recent and better,) 207.

2. Another book which promises to give some clue to its date is the *de Pallio*. The writer uses these phrases: "præsentis imperii *triplex virtus*;" "Deo *tot Augustis in unum* favente;" which show that there were at the time three persons unitedly bearing the title *Augusti*—not *Cæsares* only, but the still higher *Augusti*;—while the remainder of that context, as well as the opening of c. 1, indicates a time of peace of some considerable duration; a time of plenty; and a time during and previous to which great changes had taken place in the general aspect of the Roman Empire, and some particular traitor had been discovered and frustrated. Such a combination of circumstances might seem to fix the date with some degree of assurance. But unhappily, as Kaye reminds us, commentators cannot agree as to who the three Augusti are. Some say

Severus, Caracalla, and *Albinus*; some say Severus, Caracalla, and *Geta*. Hence we have a difference of some twelve years or thereabouts in the computations. For Albinus was defeated by Severus in person, and fell by his own hand, in a.d. 197; and Geta, Severus' second son, brother of Caracalla, was not associated by his father with himself and his other son as *Augustus* until a.d. 208, though he had received the title of *Cæsar* ten years before, in the same year in which *Caracalla* had received that of Augustus. For my own part, I may perhaps be allowed to say that I should incline to agree, like Salmasius, with those who assign the later date. The limits of the present Introduction forbid my entering at large into my reasons for so doing. I am, however, supported in it by the authority of Neander. In one point, though, I should hesitate to agree with Oehler, who appears to follow Salmasius and others herein,— namely, in understanding the expression "et cacto et rubo subdolæ familiaritatis convulso" of *Albinus*. It seems to me the words might with more propriety be applied to *Plautianus*; and that in the word "familiaritatis" we may see (after Tertullian's fashion) a play upon the meaning, with a reference not only to the long-standing but mischievous *intimacy* which existed between Severus and his countryman (perhaps fellow-townsman) Plautianus, who for his harshness and cruelty is fitly compared to the prickly *cactus*. He alludes likewise to the alliance which this ambitious prætorian præfect had contrived to contract with the *family* of the emperor, by the marriage of his daughter Plautilla to Caracalla,—an event which, as it turned out, led to his own death. Thus in the "*rubo*" there may be a reference to the ambitious and conceited "bramble" of Jotham's parable, and perhaps, too, to the "thistle" of Jehoash's. If this be so, the date would be at least approximately fixed, as Plautianus did not marry his daughter to Caracalla till a.d. 203, and was himself put to death in the following year, 204, while Geta, as we have seen, was made Augustus in 208.

3. The date of the *Apology*, however, is perhaps at once the most contested, and the most strikingly illustrative of the difficulties to which allusion has been made. It is not surprising that its date *should* have been more disputed than that of other pieces, inasmuch as it is the best known, and (for some reasons) the most interesting and famous, of all our author's productions. In fact, the dates assigned to it by different authorities vary from Mosheim's 198 to that suggested by the very learned Allix, who assigns it to 217.

4. Once more. In the tract *de Monogamia* (c. 3) the author says that since the date of St. Paul's first Epistle to the Corinthians "about 160 years had elapsed." Here, again, did we only know with certainty the precise date of that epistle, we could ascertain "about" the date of the tract. But (a) the date of the epistle is itself variously given, Burton giving it as early as a.d. 52, Michaelis and Mill as late as 57; and (b) Tertullian only says, "Armis *circiter* clx. exinde productis;" while the way in which, in the *ad Natt.*, within the short space of three chapters, he states first that 250, and then (in c. 9) that 300, years had not elapsed since the rise of the Christian name, leads us to think that here again he only desires to speak in round numbers, meaning perhaps *more* than 150, but *less* than 170.

These specimens must suffice, though it might be easy to add to them. There is, however, another classification of our author's writings which has been attempted. Finding the haplessness of strict chronological accuracy, commentators have seized on the idea that peradventure there might be found at all events some internal marks by which to determine which of them were written before, which after, the writer's secession to Montanism. It may be confessed that this attempt has been somewhat more successful than the other. Yet even here there are two formidable obstacles standing in our way. The first and greatest is, that the natural temper of Tertullian was from the first so akin to the spirit of Montanism, that, unless there occur distinct allusions to the "New Prophecy," or expressions specially connected with Montanistic phraseology, the *general tone* of any treatise is not a very safe guide. The second is, that the subject-matter of some of the treatises is not such as to afford much scope for the introduction of the peculiarities of a sect which professed to differ in discipline only, not doctrine, from the church at large.

Still the result of this classification seems to show one important feature of agreement between commentators, however they may differ upon details; and that is, that considerably the larger part of our author's rather voluminous productions must have been subsequent to his lamented secession. I think the best way to give the reader means for forming his own judgment will be, as I have said, to lay before him in parallel columns a tabular view of the disposition of the books by Dr. Neander and Bishop Kaye. These two modern writers, having given particular care to the subject, bringing to bear upon it all the advantages derived from wide reading, eminent abilities, and a diligent study of the works of preceding writers on the same questions, have a special right to be heard upon the matter in hand; and I think, if I may be allowed to say so, that, for calm judgment, and minute acquaintance with his author, I shall not be accused of undue partiality if I express my opinion that, as far as my own observation goes, the palm must be awarded to the Bishop. In this view I am supported by the fact that the accomplished Professor Ramsay, follows Dr. Kaye's arrangement. I premise that Dr. Neander adopts a threefold division, into:

1. Writings which were occasioned by the relation of the Christians to the heathen, and refer to their vindication of Christianity against the heathen; attacks on heathenism; the sufferings and conduct of Christians under persecution; and the intercourse of Christians with heathens:
2. Writings which relate to Christian and church life, and to ecclesiastical discipline:
3. The dogmatic and dogmatico-controversial treatises. And under each head he subdivides into:

a. Pre-Montanist writings; b. Post-Montanist writings: thus leaving no room for what Kaye calls "works respecting which nothing certain can be pronounced." For the sake of clearness, this order has not been followed in the table. On the other side, it will be seen that Dr. Kaye, while not assuming to speak with more than a reasonable probability, is careful so to arrange the treatises under each head as to show the order, so far as it is discoverable, in which the books under that head were published; i.e., if one book is quoted in another book, the book so quoted, if distinctly referred to as already before the world, is plainly anterior to that in which it is quoted. Thus, then, have:

Neander.
I. *Pre-Montanist.*
1. De Poenitentia.
2. De Oratione.
3. De Baptismo.
4. Ad Uxorem i.
5. Ad Uxorem ii.
6. Ad Martyres.
7. De Patientia.
8. De Spectaculis.
9. De Idololatria.
10. 11. Ad Nationes i. ii.
12. Apologeticus.
13. De Testimonio Animæ.
14. De Præscr. Hæreticorum.
15. De Cult. Fem. i.
16. De Cult. Fem. ii.
II. *Montanist.*
17–21. Adv. Marc. i. ii. iii. iv. v.
22. De Anima.
23. De Carne Christi.
24. De Res. Carn.
25. De Cor. Mil.

26. De Virg. Vel.
27. De Ex. Cast.
28. De Monog.
29. De Jejuniis.
30. De Pudicitia.
31. De Pallio.
32. Scorpiace.
33. Ad Scapulam.
34. Adv. Valentinianos.
35. Adv. Hermogenem.
36. Adv. Praxeam.
37. Adv. Judæos.
38. De Fuga in Persecutione.
Kaye.
I. *Pre-Montanist* (probably).
1. De Poenitentia.
2. De Oratione.
3. De Baptismo.
4. Ad Uxorem i.
5. Ad Uxorem ii.
6. Ad Martyres.
7. De Patientia.
8. Adv. Judæos.
9. De Præscr. Hæreticorum.
II. *Montanist* (certainly).
10. Adv. Marc. i.
11. Adv. Marc. ii.
12. De Anima.
13. Adv. Marc. iii.
14. Adv. Marc. iv.
15. De Carne Christi.
16. De Resurrectione Carnis.
17. Adv. Marc. v.
18. Adv. Praxeam.
19. Scorpiace.
20. De Corona Militis.

21. De Virginibus Velandis.
22. De Exhortatione Castitatis.
23. De Fuga in Persecutione.
24. De Monogamia.
25. De Jejuniis.
26. De Pudicitia.
III. *Montanist* (probably).
27. Adv. Valentinianos.
28. Ad Scapulam.
29. De Spectaculis.
30. De Idololatria.
31. De Cultu Feminarum i.
32. De Cultu Feminarum ii.
IV. *Works respecting which nothing certain can be pronounced.*
33. The Apology.
34. Ad Nationes i.
35. Ad Nationes ii.
36. De Testimonio Animæ.
37. De Pallio.
38. Adv. Hermogenem.

A comparison of these two lists will show that the difference between the two great authorities is, as Kaye remarks, "not great; and with respect to some of the tracts on which we differ, the learned author expresses himself with great diffidence." The main difference, in fact, is that which affects two tracts upon kindred subjects, the *de Spectaculis,* and *Idololatria,* the *de Cultu Feminarum* (a subject akin to the other two), and the *adv. Judæos*. With reference to all these, except the last, to which I believe the Archdeacon does not once refer, the Bishop's opinion appears to have the support of Archdeacon Evans, whose learned and interesting essay, referred to in the note, appears in a volume published in 1837. Dr. Kaye's Lectures, on which his book is founded, were delivered in 1825. Of the date of his first edition I am not aware. Dr. Neander's *Antignostikus* also first appeared in 1825.

The Apology

The preface to his second edition bears date July 1, 1849. As to the *adv. Judæos*, I confess I agree with Neander in thinking that, at all events from the beginning of c. 9, it is spurious. If it be urged that Jerome expressly quotes it as Tertullian's, I reply, Jerome so quotes it, I believe, when he is expounding *Daniel*. Now all that the *adv. Jud.* has to say about *Daniel* ends with the end of c. 8. It is therefore quite compatible with the fact thus stated to recognize the earlier half of the book as genuine, and to reject the rest, beginning, as it happens, just after the eighth chapter, as spurious. Perhaps Dr. Neander's Jewish birth and training peculiarly fit him to be heard on this question. Nor do I think Professor Ramsay (in the article above alluded to) has quite seen the force of Kaye's own remarks on Neander. What he does say is equally creditable to his candor and his accuracy; namely: "The instances alleged by Dr. Neander, in proof of this position, are undoubtedly very remarkable; but if the concluding chapters of the tract are spurious, no ground seems to be left for asserting that the genuine portion was posterior to the third Book against Marcion,—and none, consequently, for asserting that it was written by a Montanist." With which remark I must draw these observations on the genuine extant works of Tertullian to a close.

    The next point to which a brief reference must be made is the *lost works* of Tertullian, lists of these are given both by Oehler and by Kaye, viz.:

    1. A Book on Aaron's Robes: mentioned by Jerome, Epist. 128, *ad Fabiolam de Veste Sacerdotali* (tom. ii. p. 586, Opp. ed. Bened.).

    2. A Book on the Superstition of the Age.

    3. A Book on the Submission of the Soul.

    4. A Book on the Flesh and the Soul.

    Nos. 2, 3, and 4 are known only by their titles, which are found in the Index to Tertullian's works given in the *Codex Agobardi*; but the tracts themselves are not extant in the ms., which appears to have once contained—

5. A Book on Paradise, named in the Index, and referred to in *de Anima* 55, *adv. Marc.* iii. 12; and

6. A Book on the Hope of the Faithful: also named in the Index, and referred to *adv. Marc.* iii. 24; and by Jerome in his account of Papias, and on Ezek. xxxvi.; and by Gennadius of Marseilles.

7. Six Books on Ecstasy, with a seventh in reply to Apollonius: see Jerome. See, too, J. A. Fabricius on the words of the unknown author whom the Jesuit Sirmond edited under the name *Prædestinatus*; who gathers thence that "Soter, pope of the City, and Apollonius, bishop of the Ephesians, wrote a book against the Montanists; *in reply to whom* Tertullian, a Carthaginian presbyter, wrote." J. Pamelius thinks these seven books were originally published *in Greek*.

8. A Book in reply to the Apellesites (i.e. the followers of Apelles): referred to in *de Carne Christi*, c. 8.

9. A Book on the Origin of the Soul, in reply to Hermogenes: referred to in *de Anima*, cc. 1, 3, 22, 24.

10. A Book on Fate: referred to by Fulgentius Planciades, p. 562, Merc.; also referred to as either written, or intended to be written, by Tertullian himself, *de Anima*, c. 20. Jerome states that there was extant, or had been extant, a book on Fate under the name of Minucius Felix, written indeed by a perspicuous author, but not in the style of Minucius Felix. This, Pamelius judged, should perhaps be rather ascribed to Tertullian.

11. A Book on the Trinity. Jerome says: "Novatian wrote....a large volume on the Trinity, *as if making an epitome of a work of Tertullian's, which most men not knowing regard it as Cyprian's*." Novatian's book stood in Tertullian's name in the mss. of J. Gangneius, who was the first to edit it; in a Malmesbury ms. which Sig. Gelenius used; and in others.

12. A Book addressed to a Philosophic Friend on the Straits of Matrimony. Both Kaye and Oehler are in doubt whether Jerome's words, by which some have been led to conclude that Tertullian wrote some book or books on this and kindred subjects, really imply as much, or whether they may

not refer merely to those tracts and passages in his extant writings which touch upon such matters. Kaye hesitates to think that the "Book to a Philosophic Friend" is the same as the *de Exhortatione Castitatis*, because Jerome says Tertullian wrote on the subject of celibacy "*in his youth;*" but as Cave takes what Jerome elsewhere says of Tertullian's leaving the Church "*about the middle of his age*" to mean his *spiritual age*, the same sense might attach to his words here too, and thus obviate the Bishop's difficulty.

There are some other works which have been attributed to Tertullian—on Circumcision; on Animals Clean and Unclean; on the truth that God is a Judge—which Oehler likewise rejects, believing that the expressions of Jerome refer only to passages in the *Anti-Marcion* and other extant works. To Novatian Jerome does ascribe a distinct work on Circumcision, and this may (comp. 11, just above) have given rise to the view that Tertullian had written one also.

There were, moreover, three treatises at least written by Tertullian *in Greek*. They are:
1. A Book on Public Shows. See *de Cor.* c. 6.
2. A Book on Baptism. See *de Bapt.* c. 15.
3. A Book on the Veiling of Virgins. See de *V. V.* c. 1.

Oehler adds that J. Pamelius, in his epistle dedicatory to Philip II. of Spain, makes mention of a *Greek copy* of Tertullian in the library of that king. This report, however, since nothing has ever been seen or heard of the said copy from that time, Oehler judges to be erroneous.

It remains briefly to notice the confessedly spurious works which the editions of Tertullian generally have appended to them. With these Kaye does not deal. The fragment, *adv. omnes Hæreses*, Oehler attributes to Victorinus Petavionensis, i.e., Victorinus bishop of Pettaw, on the Drave, in Austrian Styria. It was once thought he ought to be called *Pictaviensis*, i.e. of *Poictiers*; but John Launoy has shown this to be an error. Victorinus is said by Jerome to have "understood Greek better than Latin; hence his works are excellent for the sense, but mean as to the style." Cave believes him to have been a Greek by birth. Cassiodorus states him to have been once a professor of rhetoric. Jerome's statement agrees with the style of the tract in question; and Jerome distinctly says Victorinus did write *adversus omnes Hæreses*. Allix leaves the question of its authorship quite uncertain. If Victorinus be the author, the book falls clearly within the Ante-Nicene period; for Victorinus fell a martyr in the Diocletian persecution, probably about a.d. 303.

The next fragment—"Of the Execrable Gods of the Heathens"—is of quite uncertain authorship. Oehler would attribute it "to some declaimer not quite ignorant of Tertullian's writings," but certainly not to Tertullian himself.

Lastly we come to the metrical fragments. Concerning these, it is perhaps impossible to assign them to their rightful owners. Oehler has not troubled himself much about them; but he seems to regard the *Jonah* as worthy of more regard than the rest, for he seems to have intended giving more labor to its editing at some future time. Whether he has ever done so, or given us his German version of Tertullian's own works, which, "si Deus adjuverit," he distinctly promises in his preface, I do not know. Perhaps the best thing to be done under the circumstances is to give the judgment of the learned Peter Allix. It may be premised that by the celebrated George Fabricius—who published his great work, *Poetarum Veterum Ecclesiasticorum Opera Christiana*, etc., in 1564—the *Five Books in Reply to Marcion*, and the *Judgment of the Lord*, are ascribed to Tertullian, the *Genesis* and *Sodom* to Cyprian. Pamelius likewise seems to have ascribed the *Five Books*, the *Jonah*, and the *Sodom* to Tertullian; and according to Lardner, Bishop Bull likewise attributed the *Five Books* to him.They have been generally ascribed to the Victorinus above mentioned. Tillemont, among others, thinks they may well enough be his. Rigaltius is content to demonstrate that they are not Tertullian's, but leaves the real authorship without attempting to decide it. Of the others the same eminent critic says, "They seem to have been written at Carthage, at an age not far removed from Tertullian's." Allix, after observing that Pamelius is inconsistent with himself in attributing the *Genesis* and *Sodom* at one time to Tertullian, at another to Cyprian, rejects both views equally, and assigns the Genesis with some confidence to Salvian, a presbyter of Marseilles, whose "floruit" Cave gives *cir.* 440, a contemporary of Gennadius, and a copious author. To this it is, Allix thinks, that Gennadius alludes in his *Catalogue of Illustrious Men*, c. 77.

The *Judgment of the Lord* Allix ascribes to one Verecundus, an African bishop, whose date he finds it difficult to decide exactly. He refers to two of the name: one Bishop of Tunis, whom Victor of Tunis in his chronicle mentions as having died in exile at Chalcedon a.d. 552; the other Bishop of Noba, who visited Carthage with many others a.d. 482, at the summons of King Huneric, to answer there for their faith;— and would ascribe the poem to the former, thinking that he finds an allusion to it in the article upon that Verecundus in the *de Viris Illustribus* of Isidore of Seville. Oehler agrees with him. The *Five Books* Allix seems to hint may be attributed to some imitator of the Victorinus of Pettaw named above. Oehler attributes them rather to one Victorinus, or Victor, of Marseilles, a rhetorician, who died a.d. 450. He appears in G. Fabricius as Claudius Marius Victorinus, writer of a *Commentary on Genesis*, and an epistle *ad Salomonem Abbata*, both in verse, and of some considerable length.

Apology.

THE APOLOGY.

Chapter I.

Rulers of the Roman Empire, if, seated for the administration of justice on your lofty tribunal, under the gaze of every eye, and occupying there all but the highest position in the state, you may not openly inquire into and sift before the world the real truth in regard to the charges made against the Christians; if in this case alone you are afraid or ashamed to exercise your authority in making public inquiry with the carefulness which becomes justice; if, finally, the extreme severities inflicted on our people in recently private judgments, stand in the way of our being permitted to defend ourselves before you, you cannot surely forbid the Truth to reach your ears by the secret pathway of a noiseless book. She has no appeals to make to you in regard of her condition, for that does not excite her wonder. She knows that she is but a sojourner on the earth, and that among strangers she naturally finds foes; and more than this, that her origin, her dwelling-place, her hope, her recompense, her honors, are above. One thing, meanwhile, she anxiously desires of earthly rulers—not to be condemned unknown. What harm can it do to the laws, supreme in their domain, to give her a hearing? Nay, for that part of it, will not their absolute supremacy be more conspicuous in their condemning her, even after she has made her plea? But if, unheard, sentence is pronounced against her, besides the odium of an unjust deed, you will incur the merited suspicion of doing it with some idea that it is unjust, as not wishing to hear what you may not be able to hear and condemn. We lay this before you as the first ground on which we urge that your hatred to the name of Christian is unjust. And the very reason which seems

to excuse this injustice (I mean ignorance) at once aggravates
and convicts it. For what is there more unfair than to hate a
thing of which you know nothing, even though it deserve to be
hated? Hatred is only merited when it is *known* to be merited.
But without that knowledge, whence is its justice to be
vindicated? for that is to be proved, not from the mere fact that
an aversion exists, but from acquaintance with the subject.
When men, then, give way to a dislike simply because they are
entirely ignorant of the nature of the thing disliked, why may it
not be precisely the very sort of thing they should not dislike?
So we maintain that they are both ignorant while they hate us,
and hate us unrighteously while they continue in ignorance, the
one thing being the result of the other either way of it. The
proof of their ignorance, at once condemning and excusing
their injustice, is this, that those who once hated Christianity
because they knew nothing about it, no sooner come to know it
than they all lay down at once their enmity. From being its
haters they become its disciples. By simply getting acquainted
with it, they begin now to hate what they had formerly been,
and to profess what they had formerly hated; and their numbers
are as great as are laid to our charge. The outcry is that the
State is filled with Christians—that they are in the fields, in the
citadels, in the islands: they make lamentation, as for some
calamity, that both sexes, every age and condition, even high
rank, are passing over to the profession of the Christian faith;
and yet for all, their minds are not awakened to the thought of
some good they have failed to notice in it. They must not allow
any truer suspicions to cross their minds; they have no desire to
make closer trial. Here alone the curiosity of human nature
slumbers. They like to be ignorant, though to others the
knowledge has been bliss. Anacharsis reproved the rude
venturing to criticize the cultured; how much more this judging
of those who know, by men who are entirely ignorant, might he
have denounced! Because they already dislike, they want to
know no more. Thus they prejudge that of which they are
ignorant to be such, that, if they came to know it, it could no

longer be the object of their aversion; since, if inquiry finds nothing worthy of dislike, it is certainly proper to cease from an unjust dislike, while if its bad character comes plainly out, instead of the detestation entertained for it being thus diminished, a stronger reason for perseverance in that detestation is obtained, even under the authority of justice itself. But, says one, a thing is not good merely because multitudes go over to it; for how many have the bent of their nature towards whatever is bad! how many go astray into ways of error! It is undoubted. Yet a thing that is thoroughly evil, not even those whom it carries away venture to defend as good. Nature throws a veil either of fear or shame over all evil. For instance, you find that criminals are eager to conceal themselves, avoid appearing in public, are in trepidation when they are caught, deny their guilt, when they are accused; even when they are put to the rack, they do not easily or always confess; when there is no doubt about their condemnation, they grieve for what they have done. In their self-communings they admit their being impelled by sinful dispositions, but they lay the blame either on fate or on the stars. They are unwilling to acknowledge that the thing is theirs, because they own that it is wicked. But what is there like this in the Christian's case? The only shame or regret he feels, is at not having been a Christian earlier. If he is pointed out, he glories in it; if he is accused, he offers no defense; interrogated, he makes voluntary confession; condemned he renders thanks. What sort of evil thing is this, which wants all the ordinary peculiarities of evil—fear, shame, subterfuge, penitence, lamenting? What! is that a crime in which the criminal rejoices? to be accused of which is his ardent wish, to be punished for which is his felicity? You cannot call it madness, you who stand convicted of knowing nothing of the matter.

Chapter II.

If, again, it is certain that we are the most wicked of men, why do you treat us so differently from our fellows, that is, from other criminals, it being only fair that the same crime should get the same treatment? When the charges made against us are made against others, they are permitted to make use both of their own lips and of hired pleaders to show their innocence. They have full opportunity of answer and debate; in fact, it is against the law to condemn anybody undefended and unheard. Christians alone are forbidden to say anything in exculpation of themselves, in defense of the truth, to help the judge to a righteous decision; all that is cared about is having what the public hatred demands—the confession of the name, not examination of the charge: while in your ordinary judicial investigations, on a man's confession of the crime of murder, or sacrilege, or incest, or treason, to take the points of which we are accused, you are not content to proceed at once to sentence,—you do not take that step till you thoroughly examine the circumstances of the confession—what is the real character of the deed, how often, where, in what way, when he has done it, who were privy to it, and who actually took part with him in it. Nothing like this is done in our case, though the falsehoods disseminated about us ought to have the same sifting, that it might be found how many murdered children each of us had tasted; how many incests each of us had shrouded in darkness; what cooks, what dogs had been witness of our deeds. Oh, how great the glory of the ruler who should bring to light some Christian who had devoured a hundred infants! But, instead of that, we find that even inquiry in regard to our case is forbidden. For the younger Pliny, when he was ruler of a province, having condemned some Christians to death, and driven some from their stedfastness, being still annoyed by their great numbers, at last sought the advice of Trajan, the reigning emperor, as to what he was to do with the rest, explaining to his master that, except an obstinate disinclination to offer sacrifices, he found in the religious services nothing but meetings at early morning for singing hymns to Christ and God, and sealing home their way of life by a united pledge to be faithful to their religion, forbidding murder, adultery, dishonesty, and other crimes. Upon this Trajan wrote back that Christians were by no means to be sought after; but if they were brought before him, they should be punished. O miserable deliverance,—under the necessities of the case, a self-contradiction! It forbids them to be sought after as innocent, and it commands them to be punished as guilty. It is at once merciful and cruel; it passes by, and it punishes. Why dost thou play a game of evasion upon thyself, O Judgment? If thou condemnest, why dost thou not also inquire. If thou does not inquire, why dost thou not also absolve? Military stations are distributed through all the provinces for tracking robbers. Against traitors and public foes every man is a soldier; search is made even for their confederates and accessories. The Christian alone must not be sought, though he may be brought and accused before the judge; as if a search had any other end than that in view! And so you condemn the man for whom nobody wished a search to be made when he is presented to you, and who even now does not deserve punishment, I suppose, because of his guilt, but because, though forbidden to be sought, he was found. And then, too, you do not in that case deal with us in the ordinary way of judicial proceedings against offenders; for, in the case of others denying, you apply the torture to make them confess—Christians alone you torture, to make them deny; whereas, if we were guilty of any crime, we should be sure to deny it, and you with your tortures would force us to confession. Nor indeed should you hold that our crimes require no such investigation merely on the ground that you are convinced by our confession of the name that the deeds were done,—*you* who are daily wont, though you know well enough what murder is, none the less to extract from the confessed murderer a full account of how the crime was perpetrated. So

that with all the greater perversity you act, when, holding our
crimes proved by our confession of the name of Christ, you
drive us by torture to fall from our confession, that, repudiating
the name, we may in like manner repudiate also the crimes
with which, from that same confession, you had assumed that
we were chargeable. I suppose, though you believe us to be the
worst of mankind, you do not wish us to perish. For thus, no
doubt, you are in the habit of bidding the murderer deny, and of
ordering the man guilty of sacrilege to the rack if he persevere
in his acknowledgment! Is that the way of it? But if thus you do
not deal with us as criminals, you declare us thereby innocent,
when as innocent you are anxious that we do not persevere in a
confession which you know will bring on us a condemnation of
necessity, not of justice, at your hands. "I am a Christian," the
man cries out. He tells you what he is; you wish to hear from
him what he is not. Occupying your place of authority to extort
the truth, you do your utmost to get lies from us. "I am," he
says, "that which you ask me if I am. Why do you torture me to
sin? I confess, and you put me to the rack. What would you do
if I denied? Certainly you give no ready credence to others
when they deny. When we deny, you believe at once. Let this
perversity of yours lead you to suspect that there is some
hidden power in the case under whose influence you act against
the forms, against the nature of public justice, even against the
very laws themselves. For, unless I am greatly mistaken, the
laws enjoin offenders to be searched out, and not to be hidden
away. They lay it down that persons who own a crime are to be
condemned, not acquitted. The decrees of the senate, the
commands of your chiefs, lay this clearly down. The power of
which you are servants is a civil, not a tyrannical domination.
Among tyrants, indeed, torments used to be inflicted even as
punishments: with you they are mitigated to a means of
questioning alone. Keep to your law in these as necessary till
confession is obtained; and if the torture is anticipated by
confession, there will be no occasion for it: sentence should be
passed; the criminal should be given over to the penalty which

is his due, not released. Accordingly, no one is eager for the acquittal of the guilty; it is not right to desire that, and so no one is ever compelled to deny. Well, you think the Christian a man of every crime, an enemy of the gods, of the emperor, of the laws, of good morals, of all nature; yet you compel him to deny, that you may acquit him, which without him denial you could not do. You play fast and loose with the laws. You wish him to deny his guilt, that you may, even against his will, bring him out blameless and free from all guilt in reference to the past! Whence is this strange perversity on your part? How is it you do not reflect that a spontaneous confession is greatly more worthy of credit than a compelled denial; or consider whether, when compelled to deny, a man's denial may not be in good faith, and whether acquitted, he may not, then and there, as soon as the trial is over, laugh at your hostility, a Christian as much as ever? Seeing, then, that in everything you deal differently with us than with other criminals, bent upon the one object of taking from us our name (indeed, it is ours no more if we do what Christians never do), it is made perfectly clear that there is no crime of any kind in the case, but merely a name which a certain system, ever working against the truth, pursues with its enmity, doing this chiefly with the object of securing that men may have no desire to know for certain what they know for certain they are entirely ignorant of. Hence, too, it is that they believe about us things of which they have no proof, and they are disinclined to have them looked into, lest the charges, they would rather take on trust, are all proved to have no foundation, that the name so hostile to that rival power—its crimes presumed, not proved—may be condemned simply on its own confession. So we are put to the torture if we confess, and we are punished if we persevere, and if we deny we are acquitted, because all the contention is about a name. Finally, why do you read out of your tablet-lists that such a man is a Christian? Why not also that he is a murderer? And if a Christian is a murderer, why not guilty, too, of incest, or any other vile thing you believe of us? In our case alone you are either ashamed or unwilling to mention the very names of our crimes—If to be called a "Christian" does not imply any crime, the name is surely very hateful, when that of itself is made a crime.

Chapter III.

What are we to think of it, that most people so blindly knock their heads against the hatred of the Christian name; that when they bear favorable testimony to any one, they mingle with it abuse of the name he bears? "A good man," says one, "is Gaius Seius, only that he is a Christian." So another, "I am astonished that a wise man like Lucius should have suddenly become a Christian." Nobody thinks it needful to consider whether Gaius is not good and Lucius wise, on this very account that he is a Christian; or a Christian, for the reason that he is wise and good. They praise what they know, they abuse what they are ignorant of, and they inspire their knowledge with their ignorance; though in fairness you should rather judge of what is unknown from what is known, than what is known from what is unknown. Others, in the case of persons whom, before they took the name of Christian, they had known as loose, and vile, and wicked, put on them a brand from the very thing which they praise. In the blindness of their hatred, they fall foul of their own approving judgment! "What a woman she was! how wanton! how gay! What a youth he was! how profligate! how libidinous!—they have become Christians!" So the hated name is given to a reformation of character. Some even barter away their comforts for that hatred, content to bear injury, if they are kept free at home from the object of their bitter enmity. The wife, now chaste, the husband, now no longer jealous, casts out of his house; the son, now obedient, the father, who used to be so patient, disinherits; the servant, now faithful, the master, once so mild, commands away from his presence; it is a high offence for anyone to be reformed by the detested name. Goodness is of less value than hatred of

Christians. Well now, if there is this dislike of the name, what blame can you attach to names? What accusation can you bring against mere designations, save that something in the word sounds either barbarous, or unlucky, or scurrilous, or unchaste? But Christian, so far as the meaning of the word is concerned, is derived from anointing. Yes, and even when it is wrongly pronounced by you "Chrestianus" (for you do not even know accurately the name you hate), it comes from sweetness and benignity. You hate, therefore, in the guiltless, even a guiltless name. But the special ground of dislike to the sect is, that it bears the name of its Founder. Is there anything new in a religious sect getting for its followers a designation from its master? Are not the philosophers called from the founders of *their* systems—Platonists, Epicureans, Pythagoreans? Are not the Stoics and Academics so called also from the places in which they assembled and stationed themselves? and are not physicians named from Erasistratus, grammarians from Aristarchus, cooks even from Apicius? And yet the bearing of the name, transmitted from the original institutor with whatever he has instituted, offends no one. No doubt, if it is proved that the sect is a bad one, and so its founder bad as well, that will prove that the name is bad and deserves our aversion, in respect of the character both of the sect and its author. Before, therefore, taking up a dislike to the name, it behoved you to consider the sect in the author, or the author in the sect. But now, without any sifting and knowledge of either, the mere name is made matter of accusation, the mere name is assailed, and a sound alone brings condemnation on a sect and its author both, while of both you are ignorant, because they have such and such a designation, not because they are convicted of anything wrong.

Chapter IV.

And so, having made these remarks as it were by way of preface, that I might show in its true colors the injustice of the public hatred against us, I shall now take my stand on the plea of our blamelessness; and I shall not only refute the things which are objected to us, but I shall also retort them on the objectors, that in this way all may know that Christians are free from the very crimes they are so well aware prevail among themselves, that they may at the same time be put to the blush for their accusations against us,—accusations I shall not say of the worst of men against the best, but now, as they will have it, against those who are only their fellows in sin. We shall reply to the accusation of all the various crimes we are said to be guilty of in secret, such as we find them committing in the light of day, and as being guilty of which we are held to be wicked, senseless, worthy of punishment, deserving of ridicule. But since, when our truth meets you successfully at all points, the authority of the laws as a last resort is set up against it, so that it is either said that their determinations are absolutely conclusive, or the necessity of obedience is, however unwillingly, preferred to the truth, I shall first, in this matter of the laws grapple with you as with their chosen protectors. Now first, when you sternly lay it down in your sentences, "It is not lawful for you to exist," and with unhesitating rigor you enjoin this to be carried out, you exhibit the violence and unjust domination of mere tyranny, if you deny the thing to be lawful, simply on the ground that you wish it to be unlawful, not because it ought to be. But if you would have it unlawful because it *ought* not to be lawful, without doubt that should have no permission of law which does harm; and on this ground, in fact, it is already determined that whatever is beneficial is legitimate. Well, if I have found what your law prohibits to be good, as one who has arrived at such a previous opinion, has it not lost its power to debar me from it, though that very thing, if it were evil, it would justly forbid to me? If your law has gone wrong, it is of human origin, I think; it has not fallen from heaven. Is it wonderful that man should err in making a law, or come to his senses in rejecting it? Did not the Lacedæmonians amend the laws of Lycurgus himself, thereby inflicting such pain on their author that he shut himself up, and doomed himself to death by starvation? Are you not yourselves every day, in your efforts to illumine the darkness of antiquity, cutting and hewing with the new axes of imperial rescripts and edicts, that whole ancient and rugged forest of your laws? Has not Severus, that most resolute of rulers, but yesterday repealed the ridiculous Papian laws which compelled people to have children before the Julian laws allow matrimony to be contracted, and that though they have the authority of age upon their side? There were laws, too, in old times, that parties against whom a decision had been given might be cut in pieces by their creditors; however, by common consent that cruelty was afterwards erased from the statutes, and the capital penalty turned into a brand of shame. By adopting the plan of confiscating a debtor's goods, it was sought rather to pour the blood in blushes over his face than to pour it out. How many laws lie hidden out of sight which still require to be reformed! For it is neither the number of their years nor the dignity of their maker that commends them, but simply that they are just; and therefore, when their injustice is recognized, they are deservedly condemned, even though they condemn. Why speak we of them as unjust? nay, if they punish mere names, we may well call them irrational. But if they punish acts, why in our case do they punish acts solely on the ground of a name, while in others they must have them proved not from the name, but from the wrong done? I am a practiser of incest (so they say); why do they not inquire into it? I am an infant-killer; why do they not apply the torture to get from me the truth? I am guilty of crimes against the gods, against the Cæsars; why am I, who am able to clear myself, not allowed to be heard on my own behalf? No law forbids the sifting of the crimes which it prohibits, for a judge never inflicts a righteous vengeance if he is not well assured that a crime has been committed; nor does a citizen render a true subjection to the law, if he does not know the nature of the thing on which the punishment is inflicted. It is not enough that a law is just, nor that the judge should be convinced of its justice; those from whom obedience is expected should have that conviction too. Nay, a law lies under strong suspicions which does not care to have itself tried and approved: it is a positively wicked law, if, unproved, it tyrannizes over men.

Chapter V.

To say a word about the origin of laws of the kind to which we now refer, there was an old decree that no god should be consecrated by the emperor till first approved by the senate. Marcus Æmilius had experience of this in reference to his god Alburnus. And this, too, makes for our case, that among you divinity is allotted at the judgment of human beings. Unless gods give satisfaction to men, there will be no deification for them: the god will have to propitiate the man. Tiberius accordingly, in whose days the Christian name made its entry into the world, having himself received intelligence from Palestine of events which had clearly shown the truth of Christ's divinity, brought the matter before the senate, with his own decision in favor of Christ. The senate, because it had not given the approval itself, rejected his proposal. Cæsar held to his opinion, threatening wrath against all accusers of the Christians. Consult your histories; you will there find that Nero was the first who assailed with the imperial sword the Christian sect, making progress then especially at Rome. But we glory in having our condemnation hallowed by the hostility of such a wretch. For anyone who knows him, can understand that not except as being of singular excellence did anything bring on it Nero's condemnation. Domitian, too, a man of Nero's type in cruelty, tried his hand at persecution; but as he had something of the human in him, he soon put an end to what he had begun, even restoring again those whom he had banished. Such as these have always been our persecutors,—men unjust, impious, base, of whom even you yourselves have no good to say, the sufferers under whose sentences you have been wont to restore. But among so many princes from that time to the present day, with anything of divine and human wisdom in them, point out a single persecutor of the Christian name. So far from that, we, on the contrary, bring before you one who was their protector, as you will see by examining the letters of Marcus Aurelius, that most grave of emperors, in which he bears his testimony that that Germanic drought was removed by the rains obtained through the prayers of the Christians who chanced to be fighting under him. And as he did not by public law remove from Christians their legal disabilities, yet in another way he put them openly aside, even adding a sentence of condemnation, and that of greater severity, against their accusers. What sort of laws are these which the impious alone execute against us—and the unjust, the vile, the bloody, the senseless, the insane? which Trajan to some extent made naught by forbidding Christians to be sought after; which neither a Hadrian, though fond of searching into all things strange and new, nor a Vespasian, though the subjugator of the Jews, nor a Pius, nor a Verus, ever enforced? It should surely be judged more natural for bad men to be eradicated by good princes as being their natural enemies, than by those of a spirit kindred with their own.

Chapter VI.

I would now have these most religious protectors and vindicators of the laws and institutions of their fathers, tell me, in regard to their own fidelity and the honor, and submission they themselves show to ancestral institutions, if they have departed from nothing—if they have in nothing gone out of the old paths—if they have not put aside whatsoever is most useful and necessary as rules of a virtuous life. What has become of the laws repressing expensive and ostentatious ways of living? which forbade more than a hundred *asses* to be expended on a supper, and more than one fowl to be set on the table at a time, and that not a fatted one; which expelled a patrician from the senate on the serious ground, as it was counted, of aspiring to be too great, because he had acquired ten pounds of silver; which put down the theatres as quickly as they arose to debauch the manners of the people; which did not permit the insignia of official dignities or of noble birth to be rashly or with impunity usurped? For I see the Centenarian suppers must now bear the name, not from the hundred asses, but from the hundred sestertia expended on them; and that mines of silver are made into dishes (it were little if this applied only to senators, and not to freedmen or even mere whip-spoilers). I see, too, that neither is a single theatre enough, nor are theatres unsheltered: no doubt it was that immodest pleasure might not be torpid in the wintertime, the Lacedæmonians invented their woollen cloaks for the plays. I see now no difference between the dress of matrons and prostitutes. In regard to women, indeed, those laws of your fathers, which used to be such an encouragement to modesty and sobriety, have also fallen into desuetude, when a woman had yet known no gold upon her save on the finger, which, with the bridal ring, her husband had sacredly pledged to himself; when the abstinence of women from wine was carried so far, that a matron, for opening the compartments of a wine cellar, was starved to death by her friends,—while in the times of Romulus, for merely tasting wine, Mecenius killed his wife, and suffered nothing for the deed. With reference to this also, it was the custom of women to kiss their relatives, that they might be detected by their breath. Where is that happiness of married life, ever so desirable, which distinguished our earlier manners, and as the result of which for about 600 years there was not among us a single divorce? Now, women have every member of the body heavy laden with gold; winebibbing is so common among them, that the kiss is never offered with their will; and as for divorce, they long for it as though it were the natural consequence of marriage. The laws, too, your fathers in their wisdom had enacted concerning the very gods themselves, you their most loyal children have rescinded. The consuls, by the authority of the senate, banished Father Bacchus and his mysteries not merely from the city, but from the whole of Italy. The consuls Piso and Gabinius, no Christians surely, forbade Serapis, and Isis, and Arpocrates, with their dog headed friend, admission into the Capitol—in the act casting them out from the assembly of the gods—overthrow their altars, and expelled them from the country, being anxious to prevent the vices of their base and lascivious religion from spreading. These, you have restored, and conferred highest honors on them. What has come to your religion—of the veneration due by you to your ancestors? In your dress, in your food, in your style of life, in your opinions, and last of all in your very speech, you have renounced your progenitors. You are always praising antiquity, and yet every day you have novelties in your way of living. From your having failed to maintain what you should, you make it clear, that, while you abandon the good ways of your fathers, you retain and guard the things you ought not. Yet the very tradition of your fathers, which you still seem so faithfully to defend, and in which you find your principal matter of accusation against the Christians—I mean zeal in the worship of the gods, the point in which antiquity has mainly erred—although you have rebuilt the altars of Serapis, now a Roman deity, and to Bacchus, now become a god of Italy, you offer up your orgies,—I shall in its proper place show that you despise, neglect, and overthrow, casting entirely aside the authority of the men of old. I go on meantime to reply to that infamous charge of secret crimes, clearing my way to things of open day.

Chapter VII.

Monsters of wickedness, we are accused of observing a holy rite in which we kill a little child and then eat it; in which, after the feast, we practice incest, the dogs—our pimps, forsooth, overturning the lights and getting us the shamelessness of darkness for our impious lusts. This is what is constantly laid to our charge, and yet you take no pains to elicit the truth of what we have been so long accused. Either bring, then, the matter to the light of day if you believe it, or give it no credit as having never inquired into it. On the ground of your double dealing, we are entitled to lay it down to you that there is no reality in the thing which you dare not expiscate. You impose on the executioner, in the case of Christians, a duty the very opposite of expiscation: he is not to make them confess what they do, but to make them deny what they are. We date the origin of our religion, as we have mentioned before, from the reign of Tiberius. Truth and the hatred of truth come into our world together. As soon as truth appears, it is regarded as an enemy. It has as many foes as there are strangers to it: the Jews, as was to be looked for, from a spirit of rivalry; the soldiers, out of a desire to extort money; our very domestics, by their nature. We are daily beset by foes, we are daily betrayed; we are oftentimes surprised in our meetings and congregations. Whoever happened withal upon an infant wailing, according to the common story? Whoever kept for the judge, just as he had found them, the gory mouths of Cyclops and Sirens? Whoever found any traces of uncleanness in their wives? Where is the man who, when he had discovered such atrocities, concealed them; or, in the act of dragging the culprits before the judge, was bribed into silence? If we always keep our secrets, when were our proceedings made known to the world? Nay, by whom could they be made known? Not, surely, by the guilty parties themselves; even from the very idea of the thing, the fealty of silence being ever due to mysteries. The Samothracian and Eleusinian make no disclosures—how much more will silence be kept in regard to such as are sure, in their unveiling, to call forth punishment from man at once, while wrath divine is kept in store for the future? If, then, Christians are not themselves the publishers of their crime, it follows of course it must be strangers. And whence have they their knowledge, when it is also a universal custom in religious initiations to keep the profane aloof, and to beware of witnesses, unless it be that those who are so wicked have less fear than their neighbors? Everyone knows what sort of thing rumor is. It is one of your own sayings, that "among all evils, none flies so fast as rumor." Why is rumor such an evil thing? Is it because it is fleet? Is it because it carries information? Or is it because it is in the highest degree mendacious?—a thing, not even when it brings some truth to us, without a taint of falsehood, either detracting, or adding, or changing from the simple fact? Nay more, it is the very law of its being to continue only while it lies, and to live but so long as there is no proof; for when the proof is given, it ceases to exist; and, as having done its work of merely spreading a report, it delivers up a fact, and is henceforth held to be a fact, and called a fact. And then no one says, for instance, "They say that it took place at Rome," or, "There is a rumor that he has obtained a province," but, "He has got a province," and, "It took place at Rome." Rumor, the very designation of uncertainty, has no place when a thing is certain. Does any but a fool put his trust in it? For a wise man never believes the dubious. Everybody knows, however zealously it is spread abroad, on whatever strength of asseveration it rests, that some time or other from someone fountain it has its origin. Thence it must creep into propagating tongues and ears; and a small seminal blemish so darkens all the rest of the story, that no one can determine whether the lips, from which it first came forth, planted the seed of falsehood, as often happens, from a spirit of opposition, or from a suspicious judgment, or from a confirmed, nay, in the case of some, an

The Apology

inborn, delight in lying. It is well that time brings all to light, as your proverbs and sayings testify, by a provision of Nature, which has so appointed things that nothing long is hidden, even though rumor has not disseminated it. It is just then as it should be, that fame for so long a period has been alone aware of the crimes of Christians. This is the witness you bring against us—one that has never been able to prove the accusation it sometime or other sent abroad, and at last by mere continuance made into a settled opinion in the world; so that I confidently appeal to Nature herself, ever true, against those who groundlessly hold that such things are to be credited.

Chapter VIII.

See now, we set before you the reward of these enormities. They give promise of eternal life. Hold it meanwhile as your own belief. I ask you, then, whether, so believing, you think it worth attaining with a conscience such as you will have. Come, plunge your knife into the babe, enemy of none, accused of none, child of all; or if that is another's work, simply take your place beside a human being dying before he has really lived, await the departure of the lately given soul, receive the fresh young blood, saturate your bread with it, freely partake. The while as you recline at table, take note of the places which your mother and your sister occupy; mark them well, so that when the dog-made darkness has fallen on you, you may make no mistake, for you will be guilty of a crime—unless you perpetrate a deed of incest. Initiated and sealed into things like these, you have life everlasting. Tell me, I pray you, is eternity worth it? If it is not, then these things are not to be credited. Even although you had the belief, I deny the will; and even if you had the will, I deny the possibility. Why then can others do it, if you cannot? why cannot you, if others can? I suppose we are of a different nature—are we Cynopæ or Sciapodes? You are a man yourself as well as the Christian: if you cannot do it, you ought not to believe it of others, for a Christian is a man as well as you. But the ignorant, forsooth, are deceived and imposed on. They were quite unaware of anything of the kind being imputed to Christians, or they would certainly have looked into it for themselves, and searched the matter out. Instead of that, it is the custom for persons wishing initiation into sacred rites, I think, to go first of all to the master of them, that he may explain what preparations are to be made. Then, in this case, no doubt he would say, "You must have a child still of tender age, that knows not what it is to die, and can smile under thy knife; bread, too, to collect the gushing blood; in addition to these, candlesticks, and lamps, and dogs—with tid-bits to draw them on to the extinguishing of the lights: above all things, you will require to bring your mother and your sister with you." But what if mother and sister are unwilling? or if there be neither the one nor the other? What if there are Christians with no Christian relatives? He will not be counted, I suppose, a true follower of Christ, who has not a brother or a son. And what now, if these things are all in store for them without their knowledge? At least afterwards they come to know them; and they bear with them, and pardon them. They fear, it may be said, lest they have to pay for it if they let the secret out: nay, but they will rather in that case have every claim to protection; they will even prefer, one might think, dying by their own hand, to living under the burden of such a dreadful knowledge. Admit that they have this fear; yet why do they still persevere? For it is plain enough that you will have no desire to continue what you would never have been, if you had had previous knowledge of it.

Chapter IX.

That I may refute more thoroughly these charges, I will show that in part openly, in part secretly, practices prevail among you which have led you perhaps to credit similar things about us. Children were openly sacrificed in Africa to Saturn as lately as the proconsulship of Tiberius, who exposed to public gaze the priests suspended on the sacred trees overshadowing their temple—so many crosses on which the punishment which justice craved overtook their crimes, as the soldiers of our country still can testify who did that very work for that proconsul. And even now that sacred crime still continues to be done in secret. It is not only Christians, you see, who despise you; for all that you do there is neither any crime thoroughly and abidingly eradicated, nor does any of your gods reform his ways. When Saturn did not spare his own children, he was not likely to spare the children of others; whom indeed the very parents themselves were in the habit of offering, gladly responding to the call which was made on them, and keeping the little ones pleased on the occasion, that they might not die in tears. At the same time, there is a vast difference between homicide and parricide. A more advanced age was sacrificed to Mercury in Gaul. I hand over the Tauric fables to their own theatres. Why, even in that most religious city of the pious descendants of Æneas, there is a certain Jupiter whom in their games they lave with human blood. It is the blood of a beast-fighter, you say. Is it less, because of that, the blood of a man? Or is it viler blood because it is from the veins of a wicked man? At any rate it is shed in murder. O Jove, thyself a Christian, and in truth only son of thy father in his cruelty! But in regard to child murder, as it does not matter whether it is committed for a sacred object, or merely at one's own self-impulse—although there is a great difference, as we have said, between parricide and homicide—I shall turn to the people generally. How many, think you, of those crowding around and gaping for Christian blood,—how many even of your rulers, notable for their justice to you and for their severe measures against us, may I charge in their own consciences with the sin of putting their offspring to death? As to any difference in the kind of murder, it is certainly the more cruel way to kill by drowning, or by exposure to cold and hunger and dogs. A maturer age has always preferred death by the sword. In our case, murder being once for all forbidden, we may not destroy even the fetus in the womb, while as yet the human being derives blood from other parts of the body for its sustenance. To hinder a birth is merely a speedier man-killing; nor does it matter whether you take away a life that is born, or destroy one that is coming to the birth. That is a man which is going to be one; you have the fruit already in its seed. As to meals of blood and such tragic dishes, read—I am not sure where it is told (it is in Herodotus, I think)—how blood taken from the arms, and tasted by both parties, has been the treaty bond among some nations. I am not sure what it was that was tasted in the time of Catiline. They say, too, that among some Scythian tribes the dead are eaten by their friends. But I am going far from home. At this day, among ourselves, blood consecrated to Bellona, blood drawn from a punctured thigh and then partaken of, seals initiation into the rites of that goddess. Those, too, who at the gladiator shows, for the cure of epilepsy, quaff with greedy thirst the blood of criminals slain in the arena, as it flows fresh from the wound, and then rush off—to whom do they belong? those, also, who make meals on the flesh of wild beasts at the place of combat—who have keen appetites for bear and stag? That bear in the struggle was bedewed with the blood of the man whom it lacerated: that stag rolled itself in the gladiator's gore. The entrails of the very bears, loaded with as yet undigested human viscera, are in great request. And you have men rifting up man-fed flesh? If you partake of food like this, how do your repasts differ from those you accuse us Christians of? And do those, who, with savage lust, seize on human bodies, do less because they devour the living? Have they less the pollution of human blood on them because they only lick up what is to turn into blood? They make meals, it is plain, not so much of infants, as of grown-up men. Blush for your vile ways before the Christians, who have not even the blood of animals at their meals of simple and natural food; who abstain from things strangled and that die a natural death, for no other reason than that they may not contract pollution, so much as from blood secreted in the viscera. To clench the matter with a single example, you tempt Christians with sausages of blood, just because you are perfectly aware that the thing by which you thus try to get them to transgress they hold unlawful. And how unreasonable it is to believe that those, of whom you are convinced that they regard with horror the idea of tasting the blood of oxen, are eager after blood of men; unless, mayhap, you have tried it, and found it sweeter to the taste! Nay, in fact, there is here a test you should apply to discover Christians, as well as the fire-pan and the censer. They should be proved by their appetite for human blood, as well as by their refusal to offer sacrifice; just as otherwise they should be affirmed to be free of Christianity by their refusal to taste of blood, as by their sacrificing; and there would be no want of blood of men, amply supplied as that would be in the trial and condemnation of prisoners. Then who are more given to the crime of incest than those who have enjoyed the instruction of Jupiter himself? Ctesias tells us that the Persians have illicit intercourse with their mothers. The Macedonians, too, are suspected on this point; for on first hearing the tragedy of OEdipus they made

mirth of the incest-doer's grief, exclaiming, ἤλαυνε εἰς τὴν

μητέρα. Even now reflect what opportunity there is for

mistakes leading to incestuous comminglings—your promiscuous looseness supplying the materials. You first of all expose your children, that they may be taken up by any compassionate passer-by, to whom they are quite unknown; or you give them away, to be adopted by those who will do better to them the part of parents. Well, some time or other, all memory of the alienated progeny must be lost; and when once a mistake has been made, the transmission of incest thence will still go on—the race and the crime creeping on together. Then, further, wherever you are—at home, abroad, over the seas—your lust is an attendant, whose general indulgence, or even its indulgence in the most limited scale, may easily and unwittingly anywhere beget children, so that in this way a progeny scattered about in the commerce of life may have intercourse with those who are their own kin, and have no notion that there is any incest in the case. A persevering and steadfast chastity has protected us from anything like this: keeping as we do from adulteries and all post-matrimonial unfaithfulness, we are not exposed to incestuous mishaps. Some of us, making matters still more secure, beat away from them entirely the power of sensual sin, by a virgin continence, still boys in this respect when they are old. If you would but take notice that such sins as I have mentioned prevail among you, that would lead you to see that they have no existence among Christians. The same eyes would tell you of both facts. But the two blindnesses are apt to go together; so that those who do not see what is, think they see what is not. I shall show it to be so in everything. But now let me speak of matters which are more clear.

Chapter X.

"You do not worship the gods," you say; "and you do not offer sacrifices for the emperors." Well, we do not offer sacrifice for others, for the same reason that we do not for ourselves,—namely, that your gods are not at all the objects of our worship. So we are accused of sacrilege and treason. This is the chief ground of charge against us—nay, it is the sum total of our offending; and it is worthy then of being inquired into, if neither prejudice nor injustice be the judge, the one of which has no idea of discovering the truth, and the other simply and at once rejects it. We do not worship your gods, because we know that there are no such beings. This, therefore, is what you should do: you should call on us to demonstrate their nonexistence, and thereby prove that they have no claim to adoration; for only if your gods were truly so, would there be any obligation to render divine homage to them. And punishment even were due to Christians, if it were made plain that those to whom they refused all worship were indeed divine. But you say, They are gods. We protest and appeal from yourselves to your knowledge; let that judge us; let that condemn us, if it can deny that all these gods of yours were but men. If even it venture to deny that, it will be confuted by its own books of antiquities, from which it has got its information about them, bearing witness to this day, as they plainly do, both of the cities in which they were born, and the countries in which they have left traces of their exploits, as well as where also they are proved to have been buried. Shall I now, therefore, go over them one by one, so numerous and so various, new and old, barbarian, Grecian, Roman, foreign, captive and adopted, private and common, male and female, rural and urban, naval and military? It were useless even to hunt out all their names: so I may content myself with a compend; and this not for your information, but that you may have what you know brought to your recollection, for undoubtedly you act as if you had forgotten all about them. No one of your gods is earlier than Saturn: from him you trace all your deities, even those of higher rank and better known. What, then, can be proved of the first, will apply to those that follow. So far, then, as books give us information, neither the Greek Diodorus or Thallus, neither Cassius Severus or Cornelius Nepos, nor any writer upon sacred antiquities, have ventured to say that Saturn was any but a man: so far as the question depends on facts, I find none more trustworthy than those —that in Italy itself we have the country in which, after many expeditions, and after having partaken of Attic hospitalities, Saturn settled, obtaining cordial welcome from Janus, or, as the Salii will have it, Janis. The mountain on which he dwelt was called Saturnius; the city he founded is called Saturnia to this day; last of all, the whole of Italy, after having borne the name of Oenotria, was called Saturnia from him. He first gave you the art of writing, and a stamped coinage, and thence it is he presides over the public treasury. But if Saturn were a man, he had undoubtedly a human origin; and having a human origin, he was not the offspring of heaven and earth. As his parents were unknown, it was not unnatural that he should be spoken of as the son of those elements from which we might all seem to spring. For who does not speak of heaven and earth as father and mother, in a sort of way of veneration and honor? or from the custom which prevails among us of saying that persons of whom we have no knowledge, or who make a sudden appearance, have fallen from the skies? In this way it came about that Saturn, everywhere a sudden and unlooked-for guest, got everywhere the name of the Heaven-born. For even the common folk call persons whose stock is unknown, sons of earth. I say nothing of how men in these rude times were wont to act, when they were impressed by the look of any stranger happening to appear among them, as though it were divine, since even at this day men of culture make gods of those whom, a day or two before, they acknowledged to be dead men by their public mourning for them. Let these notices of Saturn, brief as they are, suffice. It will thus also be proved that Jupiter is as certainly a man, as from a man he sprung; and that one after another the whole swarm is mortal like the primal stock.

Chapter XI.

And since, as you dare not deny that these deities of yours once were men, you have taken it on you to assert that they were made gods after their decease, let us consider what necessity there was for this. In the first place, you must concede the existence of one higher God—a certain wholesale dealer in divinity, who has made gods of men. For they could neither have assumed a divinity which was not theirs, nor could any but one himself possessing it have conferred it on them. If there was no one to make gods, it is vain to dream of gods being made when thus you have no god-maker. Most certainly, if they could have deified themselves, with a higher state at their command, they never would have been men. If, then, there be one who is able to make gods, I turn back to an examination of any reason there may be for making gods at all; and I find no other reason than this, that the great God has need of their ministrations and aids in performing the offices of Deity. But first it is an unworthy idea that He should need the help of a man, and in fact a dead man, when, if He was to be in want of this assistance from the dead, He might more fittingly have created someone a god at the beginning. Nor do I see any place for his action. For this entire worldmass—whether self-existent and uncreated, as Pythagoras maintains, or brought into being by a creator's hands, as Plato holds—was manifestly, once for all in its original construction, disposed, and furnished, and ordered, and supplied with a government of perfect wisdom. That cannot be imperfect which has made all perfect. There was nothing waiting on for Saturn and his race to do. Men will make fools of themselves if they refuse to believe that from the very first rain poured down from the sky, and stars gleamed, and light shone, and thunders roared, and Jove himself dreaded the lightnings you put in his hands; that in like manner before Bacchus, and Ceres, and Minerva, nay before the first man, whoever that was, every kind of fruit burst forth plentifully from the bosom of the earth, for nothing provided for the support and sustenance of man could be introduced after his entrance on the stage of being. Accordingly, these necessaries of life are said to have been discovered, not created. But the thing you discover existed before; and that which had a pre-existence must be regarded as belonging not to him who discovered it, but to him who made it, for of course it had a being before it could be found. But if, on account of his being the discoverer of the vine, Bacchus is raised to godship, Lucullus, who first introduced the cherry from Pontus into Italy, has not been fairly dealt with; for as the discoverer of a new fruit, he has not, as though he were its creator, been awarded divine honors. Wherefore, if the universe existed from the beginning, thoroughly furnished with its system working under certain laws for the performance of its functions, there is, in this respect, an entire absence of all reason for electing humanity to divinity; for the positions and powers which you have assigned to your deities have been from the beginning precisely what they would have been, although you had never deified them. But you turn to another reason, telling us that the conferring of deity was a way of rewarding worth. And hence you grant, I conclude, that the god-making God is of transcendent righteousness,—one who will neither rashly, improperly, nor needlessly bestow a reward so great. I would have you then consider whether the merits of your deities are of a kind to have raised them to the heavens, and not rather to have sunk them down into lowest depths of Tartarus,—the place which you regard, with many, as the prison-house of infernal punishments. For into this dread place are wont to be cast all who offend against filial piety, and such as are guilty of incest with sisters, and seducers of wives, and ravishers of virgins, and boy-polluters, and men of furious tempers, and murderers, and thieves, and deceivers; all, in short, who tread in the footsteps of your gods, not one of whom you can prove free from crime or vice, save by denying that they had ever a human existence. But as you cannot deny that, you have those foul blots also as an added reason for not believing that they were made gods afterwards. For if you rule for the very purpose of punishing such deeds; if every virtuous man among you rejects all correspondence, converse, and intimacy with the wicked and base, while, on the other hand, the high God has taken up their mates to a share of His majesty, on what ground is it that you thus condemn those whose fellow-actors you adore? Your goodness is an affront in the heavens. Deify your vilest criminals, if you would please your gods. You honor them by giving divine honors to their fellows. But to say no more about a way of acting so unworthy, there have been men virtuous, and pure, and good. Yet how many of these nobler men you have left in the regions of doom! as Socrates, so renowned for his wisdom, Aristides for his justice, Themistocles for his warlike genius, Alexander for his sublimity of soul, Polycrates for his good fortune, Croesus for his wealth, Demosthenes for his eloquence. Which of these gods of yours is more remarkable for gravity and wisdom than Cato, more just and warlike than Scipio? which of them more magnanimous than Pompey, more prosperous than Sylla, of greater wealth than Crassus, more eloquent than Tullius? How much better it would have been for the God Supreme to have waited that He might have taken such men as these to be His heavenly associates, prescient as He must have surely been of their worthier character! He was in a hurry, I suppose, and straightway shut heaven's gates; and now He must surely feel ashamed at these worthies murmuring over their lot in the regions below.

Chapter XII.

But I pass from these remarks, for I know and I am going to show what your gods are not, by showing what they are. In reference, then, to these, I see only names of dead men of ancient times; I hear fabulous stories; I recognize sacred rites founded on mere myths. As to the actual images, I regard them as simply pieces of matter akin to the vessels and utensils in common use among us, or even undergoing in their consecration a hapless change from these useful articles at the hands of reckless art, which in the transforming process treats them with utter contempt, nay, in the very act commits sacrilege; so that it might be no slight solace to us in all our punishments, suffering as we do because of these same gods, that in their making they suffer as we do themselves. You put Christians on crosses and stakes: what image is not formed from the clay in the first instance, set on cross and stake? The body of your god is first consecrated on the gibbet. You tear the sides of Christians with your claws; but in the case of your own gods, axes, and planes, and rasps are put to work more vigorously on every member of the body. We lay our heads upon the block; before the lead, and the glue, and the nails are put in requisition, your deities are headless. We are cast to the wild beasts, while you attach them to Bacchus, and Cybele, and Cælestis. We are burned in the flames; so, too, are they in their original lump. We are condemned to the mines; from these your gods originate. We are banished to islands; in islands it is a common thing for your gods to have their birth or die. If it is in this way a deity is made, it will follow that as many as are punished are deified, and tortures will have to be declared divinities. But plain it is these objects of your worship have no sense of the injuries and disgraces of their consecrating, as they are equally unconscious of the honors paid to them. O impious words! O blasphemous reproaches! Gnash your teeth upon us—foam with maddened rage against us—ye are the persons, no doubt, who censured a certain Seneca speaking of your superstition at much greater length and far more sharply! In a word, if we refuse our homage to statues and frigid images, the very counterpart of their dead originals, with which hawks, and mice, and spiders are so well acquainted, does it not merit praise instead of penalty, that we have rejected what we have come to see is error? We cannot surely be made out to injure those who we are certain are nonentities. What does not exist, is in its nonexistence secure from suffering.

Chapter XIII.

"But they are gods to us," you say. And how is it, then, that in utter inconsistency with this, you are convicted of impious, sacrilegious, and irreligious conduct to them, neglecting those you imagine to exist, destroying those who are the objects of your fear, making mock of those whose honor you avenge? See now if I go beyond the truth. First, indeed, seeing you worship, someone god, and some another, of course

The Apology

you give offence to those you do not worship. You cannot continue to give preference to one without slighting another, for selection implies rejection. You despise, therefore, those whom you thus reject; for in your rejection of them, it is plain you have no dread of giving them offence. For, as we have already shown, every god depended on the decision of the senate for his godhead. No god was he whom man in his own counsels did not wish to be so, and thereby condemned. The family deities you call Lares, you exercise a domestic authority over, pledging them, selling them, changing them—making sometimes a cooking-pot of a Saturn, a firepan of a Minerva, as one or other happens to be worn down, or broken in its long sacred use, or as the family head feels the pressure of some more sacred home necessity. In like manner, by public law you disgrace your state gods, putting them in the auction-catalogue, and making them a source of revenue. Men seek to get the Capitol, as they seek to get the herb market, under the voice of the crier, under the auction spear, under the registration of the quæstor. Deity is struck off and farmed out to the highest bidder. But indeed lands burdened with tribute are of less value; men under the assessment of a poll-tax are less noble; for these things are the marks of servitude. In the case of the gods, on the other hand, the sacredness is great in proportion to the tribute which they yield; nay, the more sacred is a god, the larger is the tax he pays. Majesty is made a source of gain. Religion goes about the taverns begging. You demand a price for the privilege of standing on temple ground, for access to the sacred services; there is no gratuitous knowledge of your divinities permitted—you must buy their favors with a price. What honors in any way do you render to them that you do not render to the dead? You have temples in the one case just as in the other; you have altars in the one case as in the other. Their statues have the same dress, the same insignia. As the dead man had his age, his art, his occupation, so it is with the deity. In what respect does the funeral feast differ from the feast of Jupiter? or the bowl of the gods from the ladle of the manes? or the undertaker from the soothsayer, as in fact this latter personage also attends upon the dead? With perfect propriety you give divine honors to your departed emperors, as you worship them in life. The gods will count themselves indebted to you; nay, it will be matter of high rejoicing among them that their masters are made their equals. But when you adore Larentina, a public prostitute—I could have wished that it might at least have been Lais or Phryne—among your Junos, and Cereses, and Dianas; when you instal in your Pantheon Simon Magus, giving him a statue and the title of Holy God; when you make an infamous court page a god of the sacred synod, although your ancient deities are in reality no better, they will still think themselves affronted by you, that the privilege antiquity conferred on them alone, has been allowed to others.

Chapter XIV.

I wish now to review your sacred rites; and I pass no censure on your sacrificing, when you offer the worn-out, the scabbed, the corrupting; when you cut off from the fat and the sound the useless parts, such as the head and the hoofs, which in your house you would have assigned to the slaves or the dogs; when of the tithe of Hercules you do not lay a third upon his altar (I am disposed rather to praise your wisdom in rescuing something from being lost); but turning to your books, from which you get your training in wisdom and the nobler duties of life, what utterly ridiculous things I find!—that for Trojans and Greeks the gods fought among themselves like pairs of gladiators; that Venus was wounded by a man, because she would rescue her son Æneas when he was in peril of his life from the same Diomede; that Mars was almost wasted away by a thirteen months' imprisonment; that Jupiter was saved by a monster's aid from suffering the same violence at the hands of the other gods; that he now laments the fate of Sarpedon, now foully makes love to his own sister, recounting (to her) former mistresses, now for a long time past not so dear as she. After this, what poet is not found copying the example of his chief, to be a disgracer of the gods? One gives Apollo to king Admetus to tend his sheep; another hires out the building labors of Neptune to Laomedon. A well-known lyric poet, too—Pindar, I mean—sings of Æsculapius deservedly stricken with lightning for his greed in practising wrongfully his art. A wicked deed it was of Jupiter—if he hurled the bolt—unnatural to his grandson, and exhibiting envious feeling to the Physician. Things like these should not be made public if they are true; and if false, they should not be fabricated among people professing a great respect for religion. Nor indeed do either tragic or comic writers shrink from setting forth the gods as the origin of all family calamities and sins. I do not dwell on the philosophers, contenting myself with a reference to Socrates, who, in contempt of the gods, was in the habit of swearing by an oak, and a goat, and a dog. In fact, for this very thing Socrates was condemned to death, that he overthrew the worship of the gods. Plainly, at one time as well as another, that is, always truth is disliked. However, when rueing their judgment, the Athenians inflicted punishment on his accusers, and set up a golden image of him in a temple, the condemnation was in the very act rescinded, and his witness was restored to its former value. Diogenes, too, makes utter mock of Hercules and the Roman cynic Varro brings forward three hundred Joves, or Jupiters they should be called, all headless.

Chapter XV.

Others of your writers, in their wantonness, even minister to your pleasures by vilifying the gods. Examine those charming farces of your Lentuli and Hostilii, whether in the jokes and tricks it is the buffoons or the deities which afford you merriment; such farces I mean as Anubis the Adulterer, and Luna of the masculine gender, and Diana under the lash, and the reading the will of Jupiter deceased, and the three famishing Herculeses held up to ridicule. Your dramatic literature, too, depicts all the vileness of your gods. The Sun mourns his offspring cast down from heaven, and you are full of glee; Cybele sighs after the scornful swain, and you do not blush; you brook the stage recital of Jupiter's misdeeds, and the shepherd judging Juno, Venus, and Minerva. Then, again, when the likeness of a god is put on the head of an ignominious and infamous wretch, when one impure and trained up for the art in all effeminacy, represents a Minerva or a Hercules, is not the majesty of your gods insulted, and their deity dishonored? Yet you not merely look on, but applaud. You are, I suppose, more devout in the arena, where after the same fashion your deities dance on human blood, on the pollutions caused by inflicted punishments, as they act their themes and stories, doing their turn for the wretched criminals, except that these, too, often put on divinity and actually play the very gods. We have seen in our day a representation of the mutilation of Attis, that famous god of Pessinus, and a man burnt alive as Hercules. We have made merry amid the ludicrous cruelties of the noonday exhibition, at Mercury examining the bodies of the dead with his hot iron; we have witnessed Jove's brother, mallet in hand, dragging out the corpses of the gladiators. But who can go into everything of this sort? If by such things as these the honor of deity is assailed, if they go to blot out every trace of its majesty, we must explain them by the contempt in which the gods are held, alike by those who actually do them, and by those for whose enjoyment they are done. This it will be said, however, is all in sport. But if I add—it is what all know and will admit as readily to be the fact—that in the temples adulteries are arranged, that at the altars pimping is practiced, that often in the houses of the temple-keepers and priests, under the sacrificial fillets, and the sacred hats, and the purple robes, amid the fumes of incense, deeds of licentiousness are done, I am not sure but your gods have more reason to complain of you than of Christians. It is certainly among the votaries of your religion that the perpetrators of sacrilege are always found, for Christians do not enter your temples even in the daytime. Perhaps they too would be spoilers of them, if they worshipped in them. What then do they worship, since their objects of worship are different from yours? Already indeed it is implied, as the corollary from their rejection of the lie, that they render homage to the truth; nor continue longer in an error which they have given up in the very fact of recognizing it to be an error. Take this in first of all, and when we have offered a preliminary refutation of some false opinions, go on to derive from it our entire religious system.

Chapter XVI.

For, like some others, you are under the delusion that our god is an ass's head. Cornelius Tacitus first put this notion into people's minds. In the fifth book of his histories, beginning the (narrative of the) Jewish war with an account of the origin of the nation; and theorizing at his pleasure about the origin, as well as the name and the religion of the Jews, he states that having been delivered, or rather, in his opinion, expelled from Egypt, in crossing the vast plains of Arabia, where water is so scanty, they were in extremity from thirst; but taking the guidance of the wild asses, which it was thought might be seeking water after feeding, they discovered a fountain, and thereupon in their gratitude they consecrated a head of this species of animal. And as Christianity is nearly allied to Judaism, from this, I suppose, it was taken for granted that we too are devoted to the worship of the same image. But the said Cornelius Tacitus (the very opposite of *tacit* in telling lies) informs us in the work already mentioned, that when Cneius Pompeius captured Jerusalem, he entered the temple to see the arcana of the Jewish religion, but found no image there. Yet surely if worship was rendered to any visible object, the very place for its exhibition would be the shrine; and that all the more that the worship, however unreasonable, had no need there to fear outside beholders. For entrance to the holy place was permitted to the priests alone, while all vision was forbidden to others by an outspread curtain. You will not, however, deny that all beasts of burden, and not parts of them, but the animals entire, are with their goddess Epona objects of worship with you. It is this, perhaps, which displeases you in us, that while your worship here is universal, we do homage only to the ass. Then, if any of you think we render superstitious adoration to the cross, in that adoration he is sharer with us. If you offer homage to a piece of wood at all, it matters little what it is like when the substance is the same: it is of no consequence the form, if you have the very body of the god. And yet how far does the Athenian Pallas differ from the stock of the cross, or the Pharian Ceres as she is put up uncarved to sale, a mere rough stake and piece of shapeless wood? Every stake fixed in an upright position is a portion of the cross; we render our adoration, if you will have it so, to a god entire and complete. We have shown before that your deities are derived from shapes modeled from the cross. But you also worship victories, for in your trophies the cross is the heart of the trophy. The camp religion of the Romans is all through a worship of the standards, a setting the standards above all gods. Well, as those images decking out the standards are ornaments of crosses. All those hangings of your standards and banners are robes of crosses. I praise your zeal: you would not consecrate crosses unclothed and unadorned. Others, again, certainly with more information and greater verisimilitude, believe that the sun is our god. We shall be counted Persians perhaps, though we do not worship the orb of day painted on a piece of linen cloth, having himself everywhere in his own disk. The idea no doubt has originated from our being known to turn to the east in prayer. But you, many of you, also under pretence sometimes of worshipping the heavenly bodies, move your lips in the direction of the sunrise. In the same way, if we devote Sun-day to rejoicing, from a far different reason than Sun-worship, we have some resemblance to those of you who devote the day of Saturn to ease and luxury, though they too go

The Apology

far away from Jewish ways, of which indeed they are ignorant. But lately a new edition of our god has been given to the world in that great city: it originated with a certain vile man who was wont to hire himself out to cheat the wild beasts, and who exhibited a picture with this inscription: The God of the Christians, born of an ass. He had the ears of an ass, was hoofed in one foot, carried a book, and wore a toga. Both the name and the figure gave us amusement. But our opponents ought straightway to have done homage to this biformed divinity, for they have acknowledged gods dog-headed and lion-headed, with horn of buck and ram, with goat-like loins, with serpent legs, with wings sprouting from back or foot. These things we have discussed *ex abundanti*, that we might not seem willingly to pass by any rumor against us unrefuted. Having thoroughly cleared ourselves, we turn now to an exhibition of what our religion really is.

Chapter XVII.

The object of our worship is the One God,101 He who by His commanding word, His arranging wisdom, His mighty power, brought forth from nothing this entire mass of our world, with all its array of elements, bodies, spirits, for the glory of His majesty; whence also the Greeks have bestowed

on it the name of Κόσμος. The eye cannot see Him, though He

is (spiritually) visible. He is incomprehensible, though in grace He is manifested. He is beyond our utmost thought, though our human faculties conceive of Him. He is therefore equally real and great. But that which, in the ordinary sense, can be seen and handled and conceived, is inferior to the eyes by which it is taken in, and the hands by which it is tainted, and the faculties by which it is discovered; but that which is infinite is known only to itself. This it is which gives some notion of God, while yet beyond all our conceptions—our very incapacity of fully grasping Him affords us the idea of what He really is. He is presented to our minds in His transcendent greatness, as at once known and unknown. And this is the crowning guilt of men, that they will not recognize One, of whom they cannot possibly be ignorant. Would you have the proof from the works of His hands, so numerous and so great, which both contain you and sustain you, which minister at once to your enjoyment, and strike you with awe; or would you rather have it from the testimony of the soul itself? Though under the oppressive bondage of the body, though led astray by depraving customs, though enervated by lusts and passions, though in slavery to false gods; yet, whenever the soul comes to itself, as out of a surfeit, or a sleep, or a sickness, and attains something of its natural soundness, it speaks of God; using no other word, because this is the peculiar name of the true God. "God is great and good"—"Which may God give," are the words on every lip. It bears witness, too, that God is judge, exclaiming, "God sees," and, "I commend myself to God," and, "God will repay me." O noble testimony of the soul by nature Christian! Then, too, in using such words as these, it looks not to the Capitol, but to the heavens. It knows that there is the throne of the living God, as from Him and from thence itself came down.

Chapter XVIII.

But, that we might attain an ampler and more authoritative knowledge at once of Himself, and of His counsels and will, God has added a written revelation for the behooved of every one whose heart is set on seeking Him, that seeking he may find, and finding believe, and believing obey. For from the first He sent messengers into the world,—men whose stainless righteousness made them worthy to know the Most High, and to reveal Him,—men abundantly endowed with the Holy Spirit, that they might proclaim that there is one

God only who made all things, who formed man from the dust of the ground (for He is the true Prometheus who gave order to the world by arranging the seasons and their course),—these have further set before us the proofs He has given of His majesty in His judgments by floods and fires, the rules appointed by Him for securing His favor, as well as the retribution in store for the ignoring, forsaking and keeping them, as being about at the end of all to adjudge His worshippers to everlasting life, and the wicked to the doom of fire at once without ending and without break, raising up again all the dead from the beginning, reforming and renewing them with the object of awarding either recompense. Once these things were with us, too, the theme of ridicule. We are of your stock and nature: men are made, not born, Christians. The preachers of whom we have spoken are called prophets, from the office which belongs to them of predicting the future. Their words, as well as the miracles which they performed, that men might have faith in their divine authority, we have still in the literary treasures they have left, and which are open to all. Ptolemy, surnamed Philadelphus, the most learned of his race, a man of vast acquaintance with all literature, emulating, I imagine, the book enthusiasm of Pisistratus, among other remains of the past which either their antiquity or something of peculiar interest made famous, at the suggestion of Demetrius Phalereus, who was renowned above all grammarians of his time, and to whom he had committed the management of these things, applied to the Jews for their writings—I mean the writings peculiar to them and in their tongue, which they alone possessed, for from themselves, as a people dear to God for their fathers' sake, their prophets had ever sprung, and to them they had ever spoken. Now in ancient times the people we call Jews bare the name of Hebrews, and so both their writings and their speech were Hebrew. But that the understanding of their books might not be wanting, this also the Jews supplied to Ptolemy; for they gave him seventy-two interpreters—men whom the philosopher Menedemus, the well-known asserter of a Providence, regarded with respect as sharing in his views. The same account is given by Aristæus. So the king left these works unlocked to all, in the Greek language. To this day, at the temple of Serapis, the libraries of Ptolemy are to be seen, with the identical Hebrew originals in them. The Jews, too, read them publicly. Under a tribute-liberty, they are in the habit of going to hear them every Sabbath. Whoever gives ear will find God in them; whoever takes pains to understand, will be compelled to believe.

Chapter XIX.

Their high antiquity, first of all, claims authority for these writings. With you, too, it is a kind of religion to demand belief on this very ground. Well, all the substances, all the materials, the origins, classes, contents of your most ancient writings, even most nations and cities illustrious in the records of the past and noted for their antiquity in books of annals,— the very forms of your letters, those revealers and custodiers of events, nay (I think I speak still within the mark), your very gods themselves, your very temples and oracles, and sacred rites, are less ancient than the work of a single prophet, in whom you have the *thesaurus* of the entire Jewish religion, and therefore too of ours. If you happen to have heard of a certain Moses, I speak first of him: he is as far back as the Argive Inachus; by nearly four hundred years—only seven less—he precedes Danaus, your most ancient name; while he antedates by a millennium the death of Priam. I might affirm, too, that he is five hundred years earlier than Homer, and have supporters of that view. The other prophets also, though of later date, are, even the most recent of them, as far back as the first of your philosophers, and legislators, and historians. It is not so much the difficulty of the subject, as its vastness, that stands in the way of a statement of the grounds on which these statements rest; the matter is not so arduous as it would be tedious. It would require the anxious study of many books, and the fingers busy reckoning. The histories of the most ancient nations, such as the Egyptians, the Chaldeans, the Phoenicians, would need to be ransacked; the men of these various nations who have information to give, would have to be called in as witnesses. Manetho the Egyptian, and Berosus the Chaldean, and Hieromus the Phoenician king of Tyre; their successors too, Ptolemy the Mendesian, and Demetrius Phalereus, and King Juba, and Apion, and Thallus, and their critic the Jew Josephus, the native vindicator of the ancient history of his people, who either authenticates or refutes the others. Also the Greek censors' lists must be compared, and the dates of events ascertained, that the chronological connections may be opened up, and thus the reckonings of the various annals be made to give forth light. We must go abroad into the histories and literature of all nations. And, in fact, we have already brought the proof in part before you, in giving those hints as to how it is to be effected. But it seems better to delay the full discussion of this, lest in our haste we do not sufficiently carry it out, or lest in its thorough handling we make too lengthened a digression.

Chapter XX.

To make up for our delay in this, we bring under your notice something of even greater importance; we point to the majesty of our Scriptures, if not to their antiquity. If you doubt that they are as ancient as we say, we offer proof that they are divine. And you may convince yourselves of this at once, and without going very far. Your instructors, the world, and the age, and the event, are all before you. All that is taking place around you was fore-announced; all that you now see with your eye was previously heard by the ear. The swallowing up of cities by the earth; the theft of islands by the sea; wars, bringing external and internal convulsions; the collision of kingdoms with kingdoms; famines and pestilences, and local massacres, and widespread desolating mortalities; the exaltation of the lowly, and the humbling of the proud; the decay of righteousness, the growth of sin, the slackening interest in all good ways; the very seasons and elements going out of their ordinary course; monsters and portents taking the place of nature's forms—it was all foreseen and predicted before it came to pass. While we suffer the calamities, we read of them in the Scriptures; as we examine, they are proved. Well, the truth of a prophecy, I think, is the demonstration of its being from above. Hence there is among us an assured faith in regard to coming events as things already proved to us, for they were predicted along with what we have day by day fulfilled. They are uttered by the same voices, they are written in the same books—the same Spirit inspires them. All time is one to prophecy foretelling the future. Among men, it may be, a distinction of times is made while the fulfillment is going on: from being future we think of it as present, and then from being present we count it as belonging to the past. How are we to blame, I pray you, that we believe in things to come as though they already were, with the grounds we have for our faith in these two steps?

Chapter XXI.

But having asserted that our religion is supported by the writings of the Jews, the oldest which exist, though it is generally known, and we fully admit that it dates from a comparatively recent period—no further back indeed than the reign of Tiberius—a question may perhaps be raised on this ground about its standing, as if it were hiding something of its presumption under shadow of an illustrious religion, one which has at any rate undoubted allowance of the law, or because, apart from the question of age, we neither accord with the Jews in their peculiarities in regard to food, nor in their sacred days, nor even in their well-known bodily sign, nor in the possession of a common name, which surely behooved to be

The Apology

the case if we did homage to the same God as they. Then, too, the common people have now some knowledge of Christ, and think of Him as but a man, one indeed such as the Jews condemned, so that some may naturally enough have taken up the idea that we are worshippers of a mere human being. But we are neither ashamed of Christ—for we rejoice to be counted His disciples, and in His name to suffer—nor do we differ from the Jews concerning God. We must make, therefore, a remark or two as to Christ's divinity. In former times the Jews enjoyed much of God's favor, when the fathers of their race were noted for their righteousness and faith. So it was that as a people they flourished greatly, and their kingdom attained to a lofty eminence; and so highly blessed were they, that for their instruction God spoke to them in special revelations, pointing out to them beforehand how they should merit His favor and avoid His displeasure. But how deeply they have sinned, puffed up to their fall with a false trust in their noble ancestors, turning from God's way into a way of sheer impiety, though they themselves should refuse to admit it, their present national ruin would afford sufficient proof. Scattered abroad, a race of wanderers, exiles from their own land and clime, they roam over the whole world without either a human or a heavenly king, not possessing even the stranger's right to set so much as a simple footstep in their native country. The sacred writers withal, in giving previous warning of these things, all with equal clearness ever declared that, in the last days of the world, God would, out of every nation, and people, and country, choose for Himself more faithful worshippers, upon whom He would bestow His grace, and that indeed in ampler measure, in keeping with the enlarged capacities of a nobler dispensation. Accordingly, He appeared among us, whose coming to renovate and illuminate man's nature was pre-announced by God—I mean Christ, that Son of God. And so the supreme Head and Master of this grace and discipline, the Enlightener and Trainer of the human race, God's own Son, was announced among us, born—but not so born as to make Him ashamed of the name of Son or of His paternal origin. It was not His lot to have as His father, by incest with a sister, or by violation of a daughter or another's wife, a god in the shape of serpent, or ox, or bird, or lover, for his vile ends transmuting himself into the gold of Danaus. They are your divinities upon whom these base deeds of Jupiter were done. But the Son of God has no mother in any sense which involves impurity; she, whom men suppose to be His mother in the ordinary way, had never entered into the marriage bond. But, first, I shall discuss His essential nature, and so the nature of His birth will be understood. We have already asserted that God made the world, and all which it contains, by His Word, and Reason, and Power. It is abundantly plain that your philosophers, too, regard the Logos—that is, the Word and Reason—as the Creator of the universe. For Zeno lays it down that he is the creator, having made all things according to a determinate plan; that his name is Fate, and God, and the soul of Jupiter, and the necessity of all things. Cleanthes ascribes all this to spirit, which he maintains pervades the universe. And we, in like manner, hold that the Word, and Reason, and Power, by which we have said God made all, have spirit as their proper and essential *substratum*, in which the Word has in being to give forth utterances, and reason abides to dispose and arrange, and power is over all to execute. We have been taught that He proceeds forth from God, and in that procession He is generated; so that He is the Son of God, and is called God from unity of substance with God. For God, too, is a Spirit. Even when the ray is shot from the sun, it is still part of the parent mass; the sun will still be in the ray, because it is a ray of the sun—there is no division of substance, but merely an extension. Thus Christ is Spirit of Spirit, and God of God, as light of light is kindled. The material matrix remains entire and unimpaired, though you derive from it any number of shoots possessed of its qualities; so, too, that which has come forth out of God is at once God and the Son of God, and the two are one.

The Apology

In this way also, as He is Spirit of Spirit and God of God, He is made a second in manner of existence—in position, not in nature; and He did not withdraw from the original source, but went forth. This ray of God, then, as it was always foretold in ancient times, descending into a certain virgin, and made flesh in her womb, is in His birth God and man united. The flesh formed by the Spirit is nourished, grows up to manhood, speaks, teaches, works, and is the Christ. Receive meanwhile this fable, if you choose to call it so—it is like some of your own—while we go on to show how Christ's claims are proved, and who the parties are with you by whom such fables have been set a going to overthrow the truth, which they resemble. The Jews, too, were well aware that Christ was coming, as those to whom the prophets spoke. Nay, even now His advent is expected by them; nor is there any other contention between them and us, than that they believe the advent has not yet occurred. For two comings of Christ having been revealed to us: a first, which has been fulfilled in the lowliness of a human lot; a second, which impends over the world, now near its close, in all the majesty of Deity unveiled; and, by misunderstanding the first, they have concluded that the second—which, as matter of more manifest prediction, they set their hopes on—is the only one. It was the merited punishment of their sin not to understand the Lord's first advent: for if they had, they would have believed; and if they had believed, they would have obtained salvation. They themselves read how it is written of them that they are deprived of wisdom and understanding—of the use of eyes and ears. As, then, under the force of their pre-judgment, they had convinced themselves from His lowly guise that Christ was no more than man, it followed from that, as a necessary consequence, that they should hold Him a magician from the powers which He displayed,—expelling devils from men by a word, restoring vision to the blind, cleansing the leprous, reinvigorating the paralytic, summoning the dead to life again, making the very elements of nature obey Him, stilling the storms and walking on the sea; proving that He was the Logos of God, that primordial first-begotten Word, accompanied by power and reason, and based on Spirit,—that He who was now doing all things by His word, and He who had done that of old, were one and the same. But the Jews were so exasperated by His teaching, by which their rulers and chiefs were convicted of the truth, chiefly because so many turned aside to Him, that at last they brought Him before Pontius Pilate, at that time Roman governor of Syria; and, by the violence of their outcries against Him, extorted a sentence giving Him up to them to be crucified. He Himself had predicted this; which, however, would have signified little had not the prophets of old done it as well. And yet, nailed upon the cross, He exhibited many notable signs, by which His death was distinguished from all others. At His own free-will, He with a word dismissed from Him His spirit, anticipating the executioner's work. In the same hour, too, the light of day was withdrawn, when the sun at the very time was in his meridian blaze. Those who were not aware that this had been predicted about Christ, no doubt thought it an eclipse. You yourselves have the account of the world-portent still in your archives. Then, when His body was taken down from the cross and placed in a sepulcher, the Jews in their eager watchfulness surrounded it with a large military guard, lest, as He had predicted His resurrection from the dead on the third day, His disciples might remove by stealth His body, and deceive even the incredulous. But, lo, on the third day there a was a sudden shock of earthquake, and the stone which sealed the sepulcher was rolled away, and the guard fled off in terror: without a single disciple near, the grave was found empty of all but the clothes of the buried One. But nevertheless, the leaders of the Jews, whom it nearly concerned both to spread abroad a lie, and keep back a people tributary and submissive to them from the faith, gave it out that the body of Christ had been stolen by His followers. For the Lord, you see, did not go forth into the public gaze, lest the wicked should be delivered from their error; that faith also, destined to a great reward, might hold its ground in difficulty. But He spent forty days with some of His disciples down in Galilee, a region of Judea, instructing them in the doctrines they were to teach to others. Thereafter, having given them commission to preach the gospel through the world, He was encompassed with a cloud and taken up to heaven,—a fact more certain far than the assertions of your Proculi concerning Romulus. All these things Pilate did to Christ; and now in fact a Christian in his own convictions, he sent word of Him to the reigning Cæsar, who was at the time Tiberius. Yes, and the Cæsars too would have believed on Christ, if either the Cæsars had not been necessary for the world, or if Christians could have been Cæsars. His disciples also, spreading over the world, did as their Divine Master bade them; and after suffering greatly themselves from the persecutions of the Jews, and with no unwilling heart, as having faith undoubting in the truth, at last by Nero's cruel sword sowed the seed of Christian blood at Rome. Yes, and we shall prove that even your own gods are effective witnesses for Christ. It is a great matter if, to give you faith in Christians, I can bring forward the authority of the very beings on account of whom you refuse them credit. Thus far we have carried out the plan we laid down. We have set forth this origin of our sect and name, with this account of the Founder of Christianity. Let no one henceforth charge us with infamous wickedness; let no one think that it is otherwise than we have represented, for none may give a false account of his religion. For in the very fact that he says he worships another god than he really does, he is guilty of denying the object of his worship, and transferring his worship and homage to another; and, in the transference, he ceases to worship the god he has repudiated. We say, and before all men we say, and torn and bleeding under your tortures, we cry out, "We worship God through Christ." Count Christ a man, if you please; by Him and in Him God would be known and be adored. If the Jews object, we answer that Moses, who was but a man, taught them their religion; against the Greeks we urge that Orpheus at Pieria,

Musæus at Athens, Melampus at Argos, Trophonius in Boeotia, imposed religious rites; turning to yourselves, who exercise sway over the nations, it was the man Numa Pompilius who laid on the Romans a heavy load of costly superstitions. Surely Christ, then, had a right to reveal Deity, which was in fact His own essential possession, not with the object of bringing boors and savages by the dread of multitudinous gods, whose favor must be won into some civilization, as was the case with Numa; but as one who aimed to enlighten men already civilized, and under illusions from their very culture, that they might come to the knowledge of the truth. Search, then, and see if that divinity of Christ be true. If it be of such a nature that the acceptance of it transforms a man, and makes him truly good, there is implied in that the duty of renouncing what is opposed to it as false; especially and on every ground that which, hiding itself under the names and images of dead, the labors to convince men of its divinity by certain signs, and miracles, and oracles.

Chapter XXII.

And we affirm indeed the existence of certain spiritual essences; nor is their name unfamiliar. The philosophers acknowledge there are demons; Socrates himself waiting on a demon's will. Why not? since it is said an evil spirit attached itself specially to him even from his childhood—turning his mind no doubt from what was good. The poets are all acquainted with demons too; even the ignorant common people make frequent use of them in cursing. In fact, they call upon Satan, the demon-chief, in their execrations, as though from some instinctive soul-knowledge of him. Plato also admits the existence of angels. The dealers in magic, no less, come forward as witnesses to the existence of both kinds of spirits. We are instructed, moreover, by our sacred books how from certain angels, who fell of their own free-will, there sprang a more wicked demon-brood, condemned of God along with the

The Apology

authors of their race, and that chief we have referred to. It will for the present be enough, however, that some account is given of their work. Their great business is the ruin of mankind. So, from the very first, spiritual wickedness sought our destruction. They inflict, accordingly, upon our bodies diseases and other grievous calamities, while by violent assaults they hurry the soul into sudden and extraordinary excesses. Their marvelous subtleness and tenuity give them access to both parts of our nature. As spiritual, they can do no harm; for, invisible and intangible, we are not cognizant of their action save by its effects, as when some inexplicable, unseen poison in the breeze blights the apples and the grain while in the flower, or kills them in the bud, or destroys them when they have reached maturity; as though by the tainted atmosphere in some unknown way spreading abroad its pestilential exhalations. So, too, by an influence equally obscure, demons and angels breathe into the soul, and rouse up its corruptions with furious passions and vile excesses; or with cruel lusts accompanied by various errors, of which the worst is that by which these deities are commended to the favor of deceived and deluded human beings, that they may get their proper food of flesh-fumes and blood when that is offered up to idol-images. What is daintier food to the spirit of evil, than turning men's minds away from the true God by the illusions of a false divination? And here I explain how these illusions are managed. Every spirit is possessed of wings. This is a common property of both angels and demons. So they are everywhere in a single moment; the whole world is as one place to them; all that is done over the whole extent of it, it is as easy for them to know as to report. Their swiftness of motion is taken for divinity, because their nature is unknown. Thus they would have themselves thought sometimes the authors of the things which they announce; and sometimes, no doubt, the bad things are their doing, never the good. The purposes of God, too, they took up of old from the lips of the prophets, even as they spoke them; and they gather them still from their works, when they hear them read aloud.

Thus getting, too, from this source some intimations of the future, they set themselves up as rivals of the true God, while they steal His divinations. But the skill with which their responses are shaped to meet events, your Croesi and Pyrrhi know too well. On the other hand, it was in that way we have explained, the Pythian was able to declare that they were cooking a tortoise with the flesh of a lamb; in a moment he had been to Lydia. From dwelling in the air, and their nearness to the stars, and their commerce with the clouds, they have means of knowing the preparatory processes going on in these upper regions, and thus can give promise of the rains which they already feel. Very kind too, no doubt, they are in regard to the healing of diseases. For, first of all, they make you ill; then, to get a miracle out of it, they command the application of remedies either altogether new, or contrary to those in use, and straightway withdrawing hurtful influence, they are supposed to have wrought a cure. What need, then, to speak of their other artifices, or yet further of the deceptive power which they have as spirits: of these Castor apparitions, of water carried by a sieve, and a ship drawn along by a girdle, and a beard reddened by a touch, all done with the one object of showing that men should believe in the deity of stones, and not seek after the only true God?

Chapter XXIII.

Moreover, if sorcerers call forth ghosts, and even make what seem the souls of the dead to appear; if they put boys to death, in order to get a response from the oracle; if, with their juggling illusions, they make a pretence of doing various miracles; if they put dreams into people's minds by the power of the angels and demons whose aid they have invited, by whose influence, too, goats and tables are made to divine,— how much more likely is this power of evil to be zealous in doing with all its might, of its own inclination, and for its own objects, what it does to serve the ends of others! Or if both angels and demons do just what your gods do, where in that case is the pre-eminence of deity, which we must surely think to be above all in might? Will it not then be more reasonable to hold that these spirits make themselves gods, giving as they do the very proofs which raise your gods to godhead, than that the gods are the equals of angels and demons? You make a distinction of places, I suppose, regarding as gods in their temple those whose divinity you do not recognize elsewhere; counting the madness which leads one man to leap from the sacred houses, to be something different from that which leads another to leap from an adjoining house; looking on one who cuts his arms and secret parts as under a different furor from another who cuts his throat. The result of the frenzy is the same, and the manner of instigation is one. But thus far we have been dealing only in words: we now proceed to a proof of facts, in which we shall show that under different names you have real identity. Let a person be brought before your tribunals, who is plainly under demoniacal possession. The wicked spirit, bidden to speak by a follower of Christ, will as readily make the truthful confession that he is a demon, as elsewhere he has falsely asserted that he is a god. Or, if you will, let there be produced one of the god-possessed, as they are supposed, who, inhaling at the altar, conceive divinity from the fumes, who are delivered of it by retching, who vent it forth in agonies of gasping. Let that same Virgin Cælestis herself the rain-promiser, let Æsculapius discoverer of medicines, ready to prolong the life of Socordius, and Tenatius, and Asclepiodotus, now in the last extremity, if they would not confess, in their fear of lying to a Christian, that they were demons, then and there shed the blood of that most impudent follower of Christ. What clearer than a work like that? what more trustworthy than such a proof? The simplicity of truth is thus set forth; its own worth sustains it; no ground remains for the least suspicion. Do you say that it is done by magic, or some trick of that sort? You will not say anything of the sort, if you have been allowed the use of your ears and eyes. For what argument can you bring

Tertullian

against a thing that is exhibited to the eye in its naked reality? If, on the one hand, they are really gods, why do they pretend to be demons? Is it from fear of us? In that case your divinity is put in subjection to Christians; and you surely can never ascribe deity to that which is under authority of man, nay (if it adds aught to the disgrace) of its very enemies. If, on the other hand, they are demons or angels, why, inconsistently with this, do they presume to set themselves forth as acting the part of gods? For as beings who put themselves out as gods would never willingly call themselves demons, if they were gods indeed, that they might not thereby in fact abdicate their dignity; so those whom you know to be no more than demons, would not dare to act as gods, if those whose names they take and use were really divine. For they would not dare to treat with disrespect the higher majesty of beings, whose displeasure they would feel was to be dreaded. So this divinity of yours is no divinity; for if it were, it would not be pretended to by demons, and it would not be denied by gods. But since on both sides there is a concurrent acknowledgment that they are not gods, gather from this that there is but a single race—I mean the race of demons, the real race in both cases. Let your search, then, now be after gods; for those whom you had imagined to be so you find to be spirits of evil. The truth is, as we have thus not only shown from our own gods that neither themselves nor any others have claims to deity, you may see at once who is really God, and whether that is He and He alone whom we Christians own; as also whether you are to believe in Him, and worship Him, after the manner of our Christian faith and discipline. But at once they will say, Who is this Christ with his fables? is he an ordinary man? is he a sorcerer? was his body stolen by his disciples from its tomb? is he now in the realms below? or is he not rather up in the heavens, thence about to come again, making the whole world shake, filling the earth with dread alarms, making all but Christians wail—as the Power of God, and the Spirit of God, as the Word, the Reason, the Wisdom, and the Son of God? Mock as you like, but get the demons if you can to join you in your mocking; let *them* deny that Christ is coming to judge every human soul which has existed from the world's beginning, clothing it again with the body it laid aside at death; let *them* declare it, say, before your tribunal, that this work has been allotted to Minos and Rhadamanthus, as Plato and the poets agree; let them put away from them at least the mark of ignominy and condemnation. They disclaim being unclean spirits, which yet we must hold as indubitably proved by their relish for the blood and fumes and foetid carcasses of sacrificial animals, and even by the vile language of their ministers. Let them deny that, for their wickedness condemned already, they are kept for that very judgment-day, with all their worshippers and their works. Why, all the authority and power we have over them is from our naming the name of Christ, and recalling to their memory the woes with which God threatens them at the hands of Christ as Judge, and which they expect one day to overtake them. Fearing Christ in God, and God in Christ, they become subject to the servants of God and Christ. So at our touch and breathing, overwhelmed by the thought and realization of those judgment fires, they leave at our command the bodies they have entered, unwilling, and distressed, and before your very eyes put to an open shame. You believe them when they lie; give credit to them, then, when they speak the truth about themselves. No one plays the liar to bring disgrace upon his own head, but for the sake of honor rather. You give a readier confidence to people making confessions against themselves, than denials in their own behalf. It has not been an unusual thing, accordingly, for those testimonies of your deities to convert men to Christianity; for in giving full belief to them, we are led to believe in Christ. Yes, your very gods kindle up faith in our Scriptures, they build up the confidence of our hope. You do homage, as I know, to them also with the blood of Christians. On no account, then, would they lose those who are so useful and dutiful to them, anxious even to hold you fast, lest some day or other as Christians you might put them to the rout,—if under the power of a follower of Christ, who desires to prove to you the Truth, it were at all possible for them to lie.

Chapter XXIV.

This whole confession of these beings, in which they declare that they are not gods, and in which they tell you that there is no God but one, the God whom we adore, is quite sufficient to clear us from the crime of treason, chiefly against the Roman religion. For if it is certain the gods have no existence, there is no religion in the case. If there is no religion, because there are no gods, we are assuredly not guilty of any offence against religion. Instead of that, the charge recoils on your own head: worshipping a lie, you are really guilty of the crime you charge on us, not merely by refusing the true religion of the true God, but by going the further length of persecuting it. But now, granting that these objects of your worship are really gods, is it not generally held that there is one higher and more potent, as it were the world's chief ruler, endowed with absolute power and majesty? For the common way is to apportion deity, giving an imperial and supreme domination to one, while its offices are put into the hands of many, as Plato describes great Jupiter in the heavens, surrounded by an array at once of deities and demons. It behooves us, therefore, to show equal respect to the procurators, prefects, and governors of the divine empire. And yet how great a crime does he commit, who, with the object of gaining higher favor with the Cæsar, transfers his endeavors and his hopes to another, and does not confess that the appellation of God as of Emperor belongs only to the Supreme Head, when it is held a capital offence among us to call, or hear called, by the highest title any other than Cæsar himself! Let one man worship God, another Jupiter; let one lift suppliant hands to the heavens, another to the altar of Fides; let one—if you choose to take this view of it—count in prayer the clouds, and another the ceiling panels; let one consecrate his own life to his God, and another that of a goat. For see that you do not give a further ground for the charge of irreligion, by taking away religious liberty, and forbidding free choice of deity, so that I may no longer worship according to my inclination, but am compelled to worship against it. Not even a human being would care to have unwilling homage rendered him; and so the very Egyptians have been permitted the legal use of their ridiculous superstition, liberty to make gods of birds and beasts, nay, to condemn to death anyone who kills a god of their sort. Every province even, and every city, has its god. Syria has Astarte, Arabia has Dusares, the Norici have Belenus, Africa has its Cælestis, Mauritania has its own princes. I have spoken, I think, of Roman provinces, and yet I have not said their gods are Roman; for they are not worshipped at Rome any more than others who are ranked as deities over Italy itself by municipal consecration, such as Delventinus of Casinum, Visidianus of Narnia, Ancharia of Asculum, Nortia of Volsinii, Valentia of Ocriculum, Hostia of Satrium, Father Curis of Falisci, in honor of whom, too, Juno got her surname. In, fact, we alone are prevented having a religion of our own. We give offence to the Romans, we are excluded from the rights and privileges of Romans, because we do not worship the gods of Rome. It is well that there is a God of all, whose we all are, whether we will or no. But with you liberty is given to worship any god but the true God, as though He were not rather the God all should worship, to whom all belong.

Chapter XXV.

I think I have offered sufficient proof upon the question of false and true divinity, having shown that the proof rests not merely on debate and argument, but on the witness of the very beings whom you believe are gods, so that the point needs no further handling. However, having been led thus naturally to speak of the Romans, I shall not avoid the controversy which is invited by the groundless assertion of those who maintain that, as a reward of their singular homage to religion, the Romans have been raised to such heights of power as to have become masters of the world; and that so certainly divine are the beings they worship, that those prosper beyond all others, who beyond all others honor them. This, forsooth, is the wages the gods have paid the Romans for their devotion. The progress of the empire is to be ascribed to Sterculus, the Mutunus, and Larentina! For I can hardly think that foreign gods would have been disposed to show more favor to an alien race than to their own, and given their own fatherland, in which they had their birth, grew up to manhood, became illustrious, and at last were buried, over to invaders from another shore! As for Cybele, if she set her affections on the city of Rome as sprung of the Trojan stock saved from the arms of Greece, she herself forsooth being of the same race,— if she foresaw her transference to the avenging people by whom Greece the conqueror of Phrygia was to be subdued, let her look to it (in regard of her native country's conquest by Greece). Why, too, even in these days the *Mater Magna* has given a notable proof of her greatness which she has conferred as a boon upon the city; when, after the loss to the State of Marcus Aurelius at Sirmium, on the sixteenth before the Kalends of April, that most sacred high priest of hers was offering, a week after, impure libations of blood drawn from his own arms, and issuing his commands that the ordinary prayers should be made for the safety of the emperor already dead. O tardy messengers! O sleepy despatches! through whose fault Cybele had not an earlier knowledge of the imperial decease, that the Christians might have no occasion to ridicule a goddess so unworthy. Jupiter, again, would surely never have permitted his own Crete to fall at once before the Roman Fasces, forgetful of that Idean cave and the Corybantian cymbals, and the sweet odour of her who nursed him there. Would he not have exalted his own tomb above the entire Capitol, that the land which covered the ashes of Jove might rather be the mistress of the world? Would Juno have desired the destruction of the Punic city, beloved even to the neglect of Samos, and that by a nation of Æneadæ? As to that I know, "Here were her arms, here was her chariot, this kingdom, if the Fates permit, the goddess tends and cherishes to be mistress of the nations." Jove's hapless wife and sister had no power to prevail against the Fates! "Jupiter himself is sustained by fate." And yet the Romans have never done such homage to the Fates, which gave them Carthage against the purpose and the will of Juno, as to the abandoned harlot Larentina. It is undoubted that not a few of your gods have reigned on earth as kings. If, then, they now possess the power of bestowing empire, when they were kings themselves, from whence had they received their kingly honors? Whom did Jupiter and Saturn worship? A Sterculus, I suppose. But did the Romans, along with the native-born inhabitants, afterwards adore also some who were never kings? In that case, however, they were under the reign of others, who did not yet bow down to them, as not yet raised to godhead. It belongs to others, then, to make gift of kingdoms, since there were kings before these gods had their names on the roll of divinities. But how utterly foolish it is to attribute the greatness of the Roman name to religious merits, since it was after Rome became an empire, or call it still a kingdom, that the religion she professes made its chief progress! Is it the case now? Has its religion been the source of the prosperity of Rome? Though Numa set agoing an eagerness after superstitious observances, yet religion among the Romans was not yet a matter of images or temples. It was frugal in its ways, its rites were simple, and there were no capitols struggling to the heavens; but the altars were offhand ones of turf, and the sacred vessels were yet of Samian earthen-ware, and from these the odors rose, and no likeness of God was to be seen. For at that time the skill of the Greeks and Tuscans in image-making had not yet overrun the city with the products of their art. The Romans, therefore, were not distinguished for their devotion to the gods before they attained to greatness; and so their greatness was not the result of their religion. Indeed, how could religion make a people great who have owed their greatness to their irreligion? For, if I am not mistaken, kingdoms and empires are acquired by wars, and are extended by victories. More than that, you cannot have wars and victories without the taking, and often the destruction, of cities. That is a thing in which the gods have their share of calamity. Houses and temples suffer alike; there is indiscriminate slaughter of priests and citizens; the hand of rapine is laid equally upon sacred and on common treasure. Thus the sacrileges of the Romans are as numerous as their trophies. They boast as many triumphs over the gods as over the nations; as many spoils of battle they have still, as there remain images of captive deities. And the poor gods submit to be adored by their enemies, and they ordain illimitable empire to those whose injuries rather than their simulated homage should have had retribution at their hands. But divinities unconscious are with impunity dishonored, just as in vain they are adored. You certainly never can believe that devotion to religion has evidently advanced to greatness a people who, as we have put it, have either grown by injuring religion, or have injured religion by their growth. Those, too, whose kingdoms have become part of the one great whole of the Roman empire, were not without religion when their kingdoms were taken from them.

Chapter XXVI.

Examine then, and see if *He* be not the dispenser of kingdoms, who is Lord at once of the world which is ruled, and of man himself who rules; if He have not ordained the changes of dynasties, with their appointed seasons, who was before all time, and made the world a body of times; if the rise and the fall of states are not the work of Him, under whose sovereignty the human race once existed without states at all. How do you allow yourselves to fall into such error? Why, the Rome of rural simplicity is older than some of her gods; she reigned before her proud, vast Capitol was built. The Babylonians exercised dominion, too, before the days of the Pontiffs; and the Medes before the Quindecemvirs; and the Egyptians before the Salii; and the Assyrians before the Luperci; and the Amazons before the Vestal Virgins. And to add another point: if the religions of Rome give empire, ancient Judea would never have been a kingdom, despising as it did one and all these idol deities; Judea, whose God you Romans once honored with victims, and its temple with gifts, and its people with treaties; and which would never have been beneath your scepter but for that last and crowning offence against God, in rejecting and crucifying Christ.

Chapter XXVII.

Enough has been said in these remarks to confute the charge of treason against your re ligion: for we cannot be held to do harm to that which has no existence. When we are called therefore to sacrifice, we resolutely refuse, relying on the knowledge we possess, by which we are well assured of the real objects to whom these services are offered, under profaning of images and the deification of human names. Some, indeed, think it a piece of insanity that, when it is in our power to offer sacrifice at once, and go away unharmed, holding as ever our convictions, we prefer an obstinate persistence in our confession to our safety. You advise us, forsooth, to take unjust advantage of you; but we know whence such suggestions come, who is at the bottom of it all, and how every effort is made, now by cunning suasion, and now by merciless persecution, to overthrow our constancy. No other than that spirit, half devil and half angel, who, hating us because of his own separation from God, and stirred with envy for the favor God has shown us, turns your minds against us by an occult influence, molding and instigating them to all that perversity in judgment, and that unrighteous cruelty, which we have mentioned at the beginning of our work, when entering on this discussion. For, though the whole power of demons and kindred spirits is subject to us, yet still, as ill-disposed slaves sometimes conjoin contumacy with fear, and delight to injure those of whom they at the same time stand in awe, so is it here. For fear also inspires hatred. Besides, in their desperate condition, as already under condemnation, it gives them some comfort, while punishment delays, to have the usufruct of their malignant dispositions. And yet, when hands are laid on them, they are subdued at once, and submit to their lot; and those whom at a distance they oppose, in close quarters they supplicate for mercy. So when, like insurrectionary workhouses, or prisons, or mines, or any such penal slaveries, they break forth against us their masters, they know all the while that they are not a match for us, and just on that account, indeed, rush the more recklessly to destruction. We resist them, unwillingly, as though they were equals, and contend against them by persevering in that which they assail; and our triumph over them is never more complete than when we are condemned for resolute adherence to our faith.

Chapter XXVIII.

But as it was easily seen to be unjust to compel freemen against their will to offer sacrifice (for even in other acts of religious service a willing mind is required), it should be counted quite absurd for one man to compel another to do honor to the gods, when he ought ever voluntarily, and in the sense of his own need, to seek their favor, lest in the liberty which is his right he should be ready to say, "I want none of Jupiter's favors; pray who art thou? Let Janus meet me with angry looks, with whichever of his faces he likes; what have you to do with me?" You have been led, no doubt, by these same evil spirits to compel us to offer sacrifice for the well-being of the emperor; and you are under a necessity of using force, just as we are under an obligation to face the dangers of it. This brings us, then, to the second ground of accusation, that we are guilty of treason against a majesty more august; for you

do homage with a greater dread and an intenser reverence to
Cæsar, than Olympian Jove himself. And if you knew it, upon
sufficient grounds. For is not any living man better than a dead
one, whoever he be? But this is not done by you on any other
ground than regard to a power whose presence you vividly
realize; so that also in this you are convicted of impiety to your
gods, inasmuch as you show a greater reverence to a human
sovereignty than you do to them. Then, too, among you, people
far more readily swear a false oath in the name of all the gods,
than in the name of the single genius of Cæsar.

Chapter XXIX.

Let it be made clear, then, first of all, if those to whom
sacrifice is offered are really able to protect either emperor or
anybody else, and so adjudge us guilty of treason, if angels and
demons, spirits of most wicked nature, do any good, if the lost
save, if the condemned give liberty, if the dead (I refer to what
you know well enough) defend the living. For surely the first
thing they would look to would be the protection of their
statues, and images, and temples, which rather owe their safety,
I think, to the watch kept by Cæsar's guards. Nay, I think the
very materials of which these are made come from Cæsar's
mines, and there is not a temple but depends on Cæsar's will.
Yes, and many gods have felt the displeasure of the Cæsar. It
makes for my argument if they are also partakers of his favor,
when he bestows on them some gift or privilege. How shall
they who are thus in Cæsar's power, who belong entirely to
him, have Cæsar's protection in their hands, so that you can
imagine them able to give to Cæsar what they more readily get
from him? This, then, is the ground on which we are charged
with treason against the imperial majesty, to wit, that we do not
put the emperors under their own possessions; that we do not
offer a mere mock service on their behalf, as not believing their

safety rests in leaden hands. But you are impious in a high degree who look for it where it is not, who seek it from those who have it not to give, passing by Him who has it entirely in His power. Besides this, you persecute those who know where to seek for it, and who, knowing where to seek for it, are able as well to secure it.

Chapter XXX.

For we offer prayer for the safety of our princes to the eternal, the true, the living God, whose favor, beyond all others, they must themselves desire. They know from whom they have obtained their power; they know, as they are men, from whom they have received life itself; they are convinced that He is God alone, on whose power alone they are entirely dependent, to whom they are second, after whom they occupy the highest places, before and above all the gods. Why not, since they are above all living men, and the living, as living, are superior to the dead? They reflect upon the extent of their power, and so they come to understand the highest; they acknowledge that they have all their might from Him against whom their might is naught. Let the emperor make war on heaven; let him lead heaven captive in his triumph; let him put guards on heaven; let him impose taxes on heaven! He cannot. Just because he is less than heaven, he is great. For he himself is His to whom heaven and every creature appertains. He gets his scepter where he first got his humanity; his power where he got the breath of life. Thither we lift our eyes, with hands outstretched, because free from sin; with head uncovered, for we have nothing whereof to be ashamed; finally, without a monitor, because it is from the heart we supplicate. Without ceasing, for all our emperors we offer prayer. We pray for life prolonged; for security to the empire; for protection to the imperial house; for brave armies, a faithful senate, a virtuous people, the world at rest, whatever, as man or Cæsar, an emperor would wish. These things I cannot ask from any but

the God from whom I know I shall obtain them, both because
He alone bestows them and because I have claims upon Him
for their gift, as being a servant of His, rendering homage to
Him alone, persecuted for His doctrine, offering to Him, at His
own requirement, that costly and noble sacrifice of prayer
despatched from the chaste body, an unstained soul, a
sanctified spirit, not the few grains of incense a farthing buys—
tears of an Arabian tree,—not a few drops of wine,—not the
blood of some worthless ox to which death is a relief, and, in
addition to other offensive things, a polluted conscience, so that
one wonders, when your victims are examined by these vile
priests, why the examination is not rather of the sacrificers than
the sacrifices. With our hands thus stretched out and up to God,
rend us with your iron claws, hang us up on crosses, wrap us in
flames, take our heads from us with the sword, let loose the
wild beasts on us,—the very attitude of a Christian praying is
one of preparation for all punishment. Let this, good rulers, be
your work: wring from us the soul, beseeching God on the
emperor's behalf. Upon the truth of God, and devotion to His
name, put the brand of crime.

Chapter XXXI.

But we merely, you say, flatter the emperor, and feign
these prayers of ours to escape persecution. Thank you for your
mistake, for you give us the opportunity of proving our
allegations. Do you, then, who think that we care nothing for
the welfare of Cæsar, look into God's revelations, examine our
sacred books, which we do not keep in hiding, and which many
accidents put into the hands of those who are not of us. Learn
from them that a large benevolence is enjoined upon us, even
so far as to supplicate God for our enemies, and to beseech
blessings on our persecutors. Who, then, are greater enemies
and persecutors of Christians, than the very parties with treason
against whom we are charged? Nay, even in terms, and most
clearly, the Scripture says, "Pray for kings, and rulers, and

powers, that all may be peace with you." For when there is disturbance in the empire, if the commotion is felt by its other members, surely we too, though we are not thought to be given to disorder, are to be found in some place or other which the calamity affects.

Chapter XXXII.

There is also another and a greater necessity for our offering prayer in behalf of the emperors, nay, for the complete stability of the empire, and for Roman interests in general. For we know that a mighty shock impending over the whole earth—in fact, the very end of all things threatening dreadful woes—is only retarded by the continued existence of the Roman Empire. We have no desire, then, to be overtaken by these dire events; and in praying that their coming may be delayed, we are lending our aid to Rome's duration. More than this, though we decline to swear by the genii of the Cæsars, we swear by their safety, which is worth far more than all your genii. Are you ignorant that these genii are called "Dæmones," and thence the diminutive name "Dæmonia" is applied to them? We respect in the emperors the ordinance of God, who has set them over the nations. We know that there is that in them which God has willed; and to what God has willed we desire all safety, and we count an oath by it a great oath. But as for demons, that is, your genii, we have been in the habit of exorcising them, not of swearing by them, and thereby conferring on them divine honor.

Chapter XXXIII.

But why dwell longer on the reverence and sacred respect of Christians to the emperor, whom we cannot but look up to as called by our Lord to his office? So that on valid grounds I might say Cæsar is more ours than yours, for our God has appointed him. Therefore, as having this propriety in him, I do more than you for his welfare, not merely because I ask it of Him who can give it, or because I ask it as one who deserves to get it, but also because, in keeping the majesty of Cæsar within due limits, and putting it under the Most High, and making it less than divine, I commend him the more to the favor of Deity, to whom I make him alone inferior. But I place him in subjection to one I regard as more glorious than himself. Never will I call the emperor God, and that either because it is not in me to be guilty of falsehood; or that I dare not turn him into ridicule; or that not even himself will desire to have that high name applied to him. If he is but a man, it is his interest as man to give God His higher place. Let him think it enough to bear the name of emperor. That, too, is a great name of God's giving. To call him God, is to rob him of his title. If he is not a man, emperor he cannot be. Even when, amid the honors of a triumph, he sits on that lofty chariot, he is reminded that he is only human. A voice at his back keeps whispering in his ear, "Look behind thee; remember thou art but a man." And it only adds to his exultation, that he shines with a glory so surpassing as to require an admonitory reference to his condition. It adds to his greatness that he needs such a reminiscence, lest he should think himself divine.

Chapter XXXIV.

Augustus, the founder of the empire, would not even have the title Lord; for that, too, is a name of Deity. For my part, I am willing to give the emperor this designation, but in the common acceptation of the word, and when I am not forced to call him Lord as in God's place. But my relation to him is one of freedom; for I have but one true Lord, the God omnipotent and eternal, who is Lord of the emperor as well. How can he, who is truly father of his country, be its lord? The name of piety is more grateful than the name of power; so the heads of families are called fathers rather than lords. Far less should the emperor have the name of God. We can only profess our belief that he is that by the most unworthy, nay, a fatal flattery; it is just as if, having an emperor, you call another by the name, in which case will you not give great and unappeasable offence to him who actually reigns?—an offence he, too, needs to fear on whom you have bestowed the title. Give all reverence to God, if you wish Him to be propitious to the emperor. Give up all worship of, and belief in, any other being as divine. Cease also to give the sacred name to him who has need of God himself. If such adulation is not ashamed of its lie, in addressing a man as divine, let it have some dread at least of the evil omen which it bears. It is the invocation of a curse, to give Cæsar the name of god before his apotheosis.

Chapter XXXV.

This is the reason, then, why Christians are counted public enemies: that they pay no vain, nor false, nor foolish honors to the emperor; that, as men believing in the true religion, they prefer to celebrate their festal days with a good conscience, instead of with the common wantonness. It is, forsooth, a notable homage to bring fires and couches out before the public, to have feasting from street to street, to turn the city into one great tavern, to make mud with wine, to run in troops to acts of violence, to deeds of shamelessness to lust allurements! What! is public joy manifested by public disgrace? Do things unseemly at other times beseem the festal days of princes? Do they who observe the rules of virtue out of reverence for Cæsar, for his sake turn aside from them? Shall piety be a license to immoral deeds, and shall religion be regarded as affording the occasion for all riotous extravagance? Poor we, worthy of all condemnation! For why do we keep the votive days and high rejoicings in honor of the Cæsars with chastity, sobriety, and virtue? Why, on the day of gladness, do we neither cover our door-posts with laurels, nor intrude upon the day with lamps? It is a proper thing, at the call of a public festivity, to dress your house up like some new brothel.

However, in the matter of this homage to a lesser majesty, in reference to which we are accused of a lower sacrilege, because we do not celebrate along with you the holidays of the Cæsars in a manner forbidden alike by modesty, decency, and purity,—in truth they have been established rather as affording opportunities for licentiousness than from any worthy motive;—in this matter I am anxious to point out how faithful and true *you* are, lest perchance here also those who will not have us counted Romans, but enemies of Rome's chief rulers, be found themselves worse than we wicked Christians! I appeal to the inhabitants of Rome themselves, to the native population of the seven hills: does that Roman vernacular of theirs ever spare a Cæsar? The Tiber and the wild beasts' schools bear witness. Say now if nature had covered our hearts with a transparent substance through which the light could pass, whose hearts, all graven over, would not betray the scene of another and another Cæsar presiding at the distribution of a largess? And this at the very time they are shouting, "May Jupiter take years from us, and with them lengthen like to you,"—words as foreign to the lips of a Christian as it is out of keeping with his character to desire a change of emperor. But this is the rabble, you say; yet, as the rabble, they still are Romans, and none more frequently than they demand the death of Christians. Of course, then, the other classes, as befits their higher rank, are religiously faithful. No breath of treason is there ever in the senate, in the equestrian order, in the camp, in the palace. Whence, then, came a Cassius, a Niger, an Albinus? Whence they who beset the Cæsar between the two laurel groves? Whence they who practiced wrestling, that they might acquire skill to strangle him? Whence they who in full amour broke into the palace, more audacious than all your Tigerii and Parthenii. If I mistake not, they were Romans; that is, they were not Christians. Yet all of them, on the very eve of their traitorous outbreak, offered sacrifices for the safety of the emperor, and swore by his genius, one thing in profession, and another in the heart; and no doubt they were in the habit of calling Christians enemies of the state. Yes, and persons who are now daily brought to light as confederates or approvers of these crimes and treasons, the still remnant gleanings after a vintage of traitors, with what verdant and branching laurels they clad their door-posts, with what lofty and brilliant lamps they smoked their porches, with what most exquisite and gaudy couches they divided the Forum among themselves; not that they might celebrate public rejoicings, but that they might get a foretaste of their own votive seasons in partaking of the festivities of another, and inaugurate the model and image of their hope, changing in their minds the emperor's name. The same homage is paid, dutifully too, by those who consult astrologers, and soothsayers, and augurs, and magicians, about the life of the Cæsars,—arts which, as made known by the angels who sinned, and forbidden by God, Christians do not even make use of in their own affairs. But who has any occasion to inquire about the life of the emperor, if he have not some wish or thought against it, or some hopes and expectations after it? For consultations of this sort have not the same motive in the case of friends as in the case of sovereigns. The anxiety of a kinsman is something very different from that of a subject.

Chapter XXXVI.

If it is the fact that men bearing the name of Romans are found to be enemies of Rome, why are we, on the ground that we are regarded as enemies, denied the name of Romans? *We* may be at once Romans and foes of Rome, when men passing for Romans are discovered to be enemies of their country. So the affection, and fealty, and reverence, due to the emperors do not consist in such tokens of homage as these, which even hostility may be zealous in performing, chiefly as a cloak to its purposes; but in those ways which Deity as certainly enjoins on us, as they are held to be necessary in the case of all men as well as emperors. Deeds of true heart-goodness are not due by us to emperors alone. We never do good with respect of persons; for in our own interest we conduct ourselves as those who take no payment either of praise or premium from man, but from God, who both requires and remunerates an impartial benevolence. We are the same to emperors as to our ordinary neighbors. For we are equally forbidden to wish ill, to do ill, to speak ill, to think ill of all men. The thing we must not do to an emperor, we must not do to anyone else: what we would not do to anybody, a *fortiori*, perhaps we should not do to him whom God has been pleased so highly to exalt.

Chapter XXXVII.

If we are enjoined, then, to love our enemies, as I have remarked above, whom have we to hate? If injured, we are forbidden to retaliate, lest we become as bad ourselves: who can suffer injury at our hands? In regard to this, recall your own experiences. How often you inflict gross cruelties on Christians, partly because it is your own inclination, and partly in obedience to the laws! How often, too, the hostile mob, paying no regard to you, takes the law into its own hand, and assails us with stones and flames! With the very frenzy of the Bacchanals, they do not even spare the Christian dead, but tear them, now sadly changed, no longer entire, from the rest of the tomb, from the asylum we might say of death, cutting them in pieces, rending them asunder. Yet, banded together as we are, ever so ready to sacrifice our lives, what single case of revenge for injury are you able to point to, though, if it were held right among us to repay evil by evil, a single night with a torch or two could achieve an ample vengeance? But away with the idea of a sect divine avenging itself by human fires, or shrinking from the sufferings in which it is tried. If we desired, indeed, to act the part of open enemies, not merely of secret avengers, would there be any lacking in strength, whether of numbers or resources? The Moors, the Marcomanni, the Parthians themselves, or any single people, however great, inhabiting a distinct territory, and confined within its own boundaries, surpasses, forsooth, in numbers, one spread over all the world! We are but of yesterday, and we have filled every place among you—cities, islands, fortresses, towns, market-places, the very camp, tribes, companies, palace, senate, forum,—we have left nothing to you but the temples of your gods. For what wars should we not be fit, not eager, even with unequal forces, we who so willingly yield ourselves to the sword, if in our religion it were not counted better to be slain than to slay? Without arms even, and raising no insurrectionary banner, but simply in enmity to you, we could carry on the contest with you by an ill-willed severance alone. For if such multitudes of men were to break away from you, and betake themselves to some remote corner of the world, why, the very loss of so many citizens, whatever sort they were, would cover the empire with shame; nay, in the very forsaking, vengeance would be inflicted. Why, you would be horror-struck at the solitude in which you would find yourselves, at such an all-prevailing silence, and that stupor as of a dead world. You would have to seek subjects to govern. You would have more enemies than citizens remaining. For now it is the immense number of Christians which makes your enemies so few,—almost all the inhabitants of your various cities being followers of Christ. Yet you choose to call us enemies of the human race, rather than of human error. Nay, who would deliver you from those secret foes, ever busy both destroying your souls and ruining your health? Who would save you, I mean, from the attacks of those spirits of evil, which without reward or hire we exorcise? This alone would be revenge enough for us, that you were henceforth left free to the possession of unclean spirits. But instead of taking into account what is due to us for the important protection we afford you, and though we are not merely no trouble to you, but in fact necessary to your well-being, you prefer to hold us enemies, as indeed we are, yet not of man, but rather of his error.

Chapter XXXVIII.

Ought not Christians, therefore, to receive not merely a somewhat milder treatment, but to have a place among the law-tolerated societies, seeing they are not chargeable with any such crimes as are commonly dreaded from societies of the illicit class? For, unless I mistake the matter, the prevention of such associations is based on a prudential regard to public order, that the state may not be divided into parties, which would naturally lead to disturbance in the electoral assemblies, the councils, the curiæ, the special conventions, even in the public shows by the hostile collisions of rival parties; especially when now, in pursuit of gain, men have begun to consider their violence an article to be bought and sold. But as those in whom all ardor in the pursuit of glory and honor is dead, we have no pressing inducement to take part in your public meetings; nor is there aught more entirely foreign to us than affairs of state. We acknowledge one all-embracing commonwealth—the world. We renounce all your spectacles, as strongly as we renounce the matters originating them, which we know were conceived of superstition, when we give up the very things which are the basis of their representations. Among us nothing is ever said, or seen, or heard, which has anything in common with the madness of the circus, the immodesty of the theatre, the atrocities of the arena, the useless exercises of the wrestling-ground. Why do you take offence at us because we differ from you in regard to your pleasures? If we will not partake of your enjoyments, the loss is ours, if there be loss in the case, not yours. We reject what pleases you. You, on the other hand, have no taste for what is our delight. The Epicureans were allowed by you to decide for themselves one true source of pleasure—I mean equanimity; the Christian, on his part, has many such enjoyments—what harm in that?

Chapter XXXIX.

I shall at once go on, then, to exhibit the peculiarities of the Christian society, that, as I have refuted the evil charged against it, I may point out its positive good. We are a body knit together as such by a common religious profession, by unity of discipline, and by the bond of a common hope. We meet together as an assembly and congregation, that, offering up prayer to God as with united force, we may wrestle with Him in our supplications. This violence God delights in. We pray, too, for the emperors, for their ministers and for all in authority, for the welfare of the world, for the prevalence of peace, for the delay of the final consummation. We assemble to read our sacred writings, if any peculiarity of the times makes either forewarning or reminiscence needful. However it be in that respect, with the sacred words we nourish our faith, we animate our hope, we make our confidence more steadfast; and no less by inculcations of God's precepts we confirm good habits. In the same place also exhortations are made, rebukes and sacred censures are administered. For with a great gravity is the work of judging carried on among us, as befits those who feel assured that they are in the sight of God; and you have the most notable example of judgment to come when any one has sinned so grievously as to require his severance from us in prayer, in the congregation and in all sacred intercourse. The tried men of our elders preside over us, obtaining that honor not by purchase, but by established character. There is no buying and selling of any sort in the things of God. Though we have our treasure-chest, it is not made up of purchase-money, as of a religion that has its price. On the monthly day, if he likes, each puts in a small donation; but only if it be his pleasure, and only if he be able: for there is no compulsion; all is voluntary. These gifts are, as it were, piety's deposit fund. For they are not taken thence and spent on feasts, and drinking-bouts, and eating-houses, but to support and bury poor people, to supply the wants of boys and girls destitute of means and parents, and of old persons confined now to the house; such, too, as have suffered shipwreck; and if there happen to be any in the mines, or banished to the islands, or shut up in the prisons, for nothing but their fidelity to the cause of God's Church, they become the nurslings of their confession. But it is mainly the deeds of a love so noble that lead many to put a brand upon us. *See*, they say, *how they love one another*, for themselves are animated by mutual hatred; how they are ready even to die for one another, for they themselves will sooner put to death. And they are wroth with us, too, because we call each other brethren; for no other reason, as I think, than because among themselves names of consanguinity are assumed in mere pretence of affection. But we are your brethren as well, by the law of our common mother nature, though you are hardly men, because brothers so unkind. At the same time, how much more fittingly they are called and counted brothers who have been led to the knowledge of God as their common Father, who have drunk in one spirit of holiness, who from the same womb of a common ignorance have agonized into the same light of truth! But on this very account, perhaps, we are regarded as having less claim to be held true brothers, that no tragedy makes a noise about our brotherhood, or that the family possessions, which generally destroy brotherhood among you, create fraternal bonds among us. One in mind and soul, we do not hesitate to share our earthly goods with one another. All things are common among us but our wives. We give up our community where it is practiced alone by others, who not only take possession of the wives of their friends, but most tolerantly also accommodate their friends with theirs, following the example, I believe, of those wise men of ancient times, the Greek Socrates and the Roman Cato, who shared with their friends the wives whom they had married, it seems for the sake of progeny both to themselves and to others; whether in this acting against their partners' wishes, I am not able to say. Why should they have any care over their chastity, when their husbands so readily bestowed it away? O noble example of Attic wisdom, of Roman gravity—the philosopher and the censor playing pimps! What wonder if that great love of Christians towards one another is desecrated by you! For you abuse also our humble feasts, on the ground that they are extravagant as well as infamously wicked. To us, it seems, applies the saying of Diogenes: "The people of Megara feast as though they were going to die on the morrow; they build as though they were never to die!" But one sees more readily the mote in another's eye than the beam in his own. Why, the very air is soured with the eructations of so many tribes, and *curiæ*, and *decuriæ*. The Salii cannot have their feast without going into debt; you must get the accountants to tell you what the tenths of Hercules and the sacrificial banquets cost; the choicest cook is appointed for the Apaturia, the Dionysia, the Attic mysteries; the smoke from the banquet of Serapis will call out the firemen. Yet about the modest supper-room of the Christians alone a great ado is made. Our feast explains itself by its name. The Greeks call it *agapè*, i.e., affection. Whatever it costs, our outlay in the name of piety is gain, since with the good things of the feast we benefit the needy; not as it is with you, do parasites aspire to the glory of satisfying their licentious propensities, selling themselves for a belly-feast to all disgraceful treatment,—but as it is with God himself, a peculiar respect is shown to the lowly. If the object of our feast be good, in the light of that consider its further regulations. As it is an act of religious service, it permits no vileness or immodesty. The participants, before reclining, taste first of prayer to God. As much is eaten as satisfies the cravings of hunger; as much is drunk as befits the chaste. They say it is enough, as those who remember that even during the night they have to worship God; they talk as those who know that the Lord is one of their auditors. After manual ablution, and the bringing in of lights, each is asked to stand forth and sing, as he can, a hymn to God, either one from the holy Scriptures or one of his own composing,—a proof of the measure of our drinking. As the feast commenced with prayer, so with prayer it is closed. We go from it, not like troops of mischief-doers, nor bands of vagabonds, nor to break out into licentious acts, but to have as much care of our modesty and chastity as if we had been at a school of virtue rather than a banquet. Give the congregation of the Christians its due, and hold it unlawful, if it is like assemblies of the illicit sort: by all means let it be condemned, if any complaint can be validly laid against it, such as lies against secret factions. But who has ever suffered harm from our assemblies? We are in our congregations just what we are when separated from each other; we are as a community what we are individuals; we injure nobody, we trouble nobody. When the upright, when the virtuous meet together, when the pious, when the pure assemble in congregation, you ought not to call that a faction, but a *curia*—[i.e., the court of God.]

Chapter XL.

On the contrary, *they* deserve the name of faction who conspire to bring odium on good men and virtuous, who cry out against innocent blood, offering as the justification of their enmity the baseless plea, that they think the Christians the cause of every public disaster, of every affliction with which the people are visited. If the Tiber rises as high as the city walls, if the Nile does not send its waters up over the fields, if the heavens give no rain, if there is an earthquake, if there is famine or pestilence, straightway the cry is, "Away with the Christians to the lion!" What! shall you give such multitudes to a single beast? Pray, tell me how many calamities befell the world and particular cities before Tiberius reigned—before the coming, that is, of Christ? We read of the islands of Hiera, and Anaphe, and Delos, and Rhodes, and Cos, with many thousands of human beings, having been swallowed up. Plato informs us that a region larger than Asia or Africa was seized by the Atlantic Ocean. An earthquake, too, drank up the Corinthian sea; and the force of the waves cut off a part of

Lucania, whence it obtained the name of Sicily. These things surely could not have taken place without the inhabitants suffering by them. But where—I do not say were Christians, those despisers of your gods—but where were your gods themselves in those days, when the flood poured its destroying waters over all the world, or, as Plato thought, merely the level portion of it? For that they are of later date than that calamity, the very cities in which they were born and died, nay, which they founded, bear ample testimony; for the cities could have no existence at this day unless as belonging to postdiluvian times. Palestine had not yet received from Egypt its Jewish swarm (of emigrants), nor had the race from which Christians sprung yet settled down there, when its neighbors Sodom and Gomorrah were consumed by fire from heaven. The country yet smells of that conflagration; and if there are apples there upon the trees, it is only a promise to the eye they give—you but touch them, and they turn to ashes. Nor had Tuscia and Campania to complain of Christians in the days when fire from heaven overwhelmed Vulsinii, and Pompeii was destroyed by fire from its own mountain. No one yet worshipped the true God at Rome, when Hannibal at Cannæ counted the Roman slain by the pecks of Roman rings. Your gods were all objects of adoration, universally acknowledged, when the Senones closely besieged the very Capitol. And it is in keeping with all this, that if adversity has at any time befallen cities, the temples and the walls have equally shared in the disaster, so that it is clear to demonstration the thing was not the doing of the gods, seeing it also overtook themselves. The truth is, the human race has always deserved ill at God's hand. First of all, as undutiful to Him, because when it knew Him in part, it not only did not seek after Him, but even invented other gods of its own to worship; and further, because, as the result of their willing ignorance of the Teacher of righteousness, the Judge and Avenger of sin, all vices and crimes grew and flourished. But had men sought, they would have come to know the glorious object of their seeking; and knowledge would have produced obedience, and obedience would have found a gracious instead of an angry God. They ought then to see that the very same God is angry with them now as in ancient times, before Christians were so much as spoken of. It was *His* blessings they enjoyed—created before they made any of their deities: and why can they not take it in, that their evils come from the Being whose goodness they have failed to recognize? They suffer at the hands of Him to whom they have been ungrateful. And, for all that is said, if we compare the calamities of former times, they fall on us more lightly now, since God gave Christians to the world; for from that time virtue put some restraint on the world's wickedness, and men began to pray for the averting of God's wrath. In a word, when the summer clouds give no rain, and the season is matter of anxiety, you indeed—full of feasting day by day, and ever eager for the banquet, baths and taverns and brothels always busy—offer up to Jupiter your rain-sacrifices; you enjoin on the people barefoot processions; you seek heaven at the Capitol; you look up to the temple-ceilings for the longed-for clouds—God and heaven not in all your thoughts. We, dried up with fastings, and our passions bound tightly up, holding back as long as possible from all the ordinary enjoyments of life, rolling in sackcloth and ashes, assail heaven with our importunities—touch God's heart—and when we have extorted divine compassion, why, Jupiter gets all the honor!

Chapter XLI.

You, therefore, are the sources of trouble in human affairs; on you lies the blame of public adversities, since you are ever attracting them—you by whom God is despised and images are worshipped. It should surely seem the more natural thing to believe that it is the neglected One who is angry, and not they to whom all homage is paid; or most unjustly they act, if, on account of the Christians, they send trouble on their own devotees, whom they are bound to keep clear of the punishments of Christians. But this, you say, hits your God as well, since He permits His worshippers to suffer on account of those who dishonor Him. But admit first of all His providential arrangings, and you will not make this retort. For He who once for all appointed an eternal judgment at the world's close, does not precipitate the separation, which is essential to judgment, before the end. Meanwhile He deals with all sorts of men alike, so that all together share His favors and reproofs. His will is, that outcasts and elect should have adversities and prosperities in common, that we should have all the same experience of His goodness and severity. Having learned these things from His own lips, we love His goodness, we fear His wrath, while both by you are treated with contempt; and hence the sufferings of life, so far as it is our lot to be overtaken by them, are in our case gracious admonitions, while in yours they are divine punishments. We indeed are not the least put about: for, first, only one thing in this life greatly concerns us, and that is, to get quickly out of it; and next, if any adversity befalls us, it is laid to the door of your transgressions.

Nay, though we are likewise involved in troubles because of our close connection with you, we are rather glad of it, because we recognize in it divine foretelling, which, in fact, go to confirm the confidence and faith of our hope. But if all the evils you endure are inflicted on you by the gods you worship out of spite to us, why do you continue to pay homage to beings so ungrateful, and unjust; who, instead of being angry with you, should rather have been aiding and abetting you by persecuting Christians—keeping *you* clear of their sufferings?

Chapter XLII.

But we are called to account as harm-doers on another ground, and are accused of being useless in the affairs of life. How in all the world can that be the case with people who are living among you, eating the same food, wearing the same attire, having the same habits, under the same necessities of

The Apology

existence? We are not Indian Brahmins or Gymnosophists, who dwell in woods and exile themselves from ordinary human life. We do not forget the debt of gratitude we owe to God, our Lord and Creator; we reject no creature of His hands, though certainly we exercise restraint upon ourselves, lest of any gift of His we make an immoderate or sinful use. So we sojourn with you in the world, abjuring neither forum, nor shambles, nor bath, nor booth, nor workshop, nor inn, nor weekly market, nor any other places of commerce. We sail with you, and fight with you, and till the ground with you; and in like manner we unite with you in your trafficking—even in the various arts we make public property of our works for your benefit. How it is we seem useless in your ordinary business, living with you and by you as we do, I am not able to understand. But if I do not frequent your religious ceremonies, I am still on the sacred day a man. I do not at the Saturnalia bathe myself at dawn, that I may not lose both day and night; yet I bathe at a decent and healthful hour, which preserves me both in heat and blood. I can be rigid and pallid like you after ablution when I am dead. I do not recline in public at the feast of Bacchus, after the manner of the beast-fighters at their final banquet. Yet of your resources I partake, *wherever* I may chance to eat. I do not buy a crown for my head. What matters it to you how I use them, if nevertheless the flowers are purchased? I think it more agreeable to have them free and loose, waving all about. Even if they are woven into a crown, we smell the crown with our nostrils: let those look to it who scent the perfume with their hair. We do not go to your spectacles; yet the articles that are sold there, if I need them, I will obtain more readily at their proper places. We certainly buy no frankincense. If the Arabias complain of this, let the Sabæans be well assured that their more precious and costly merchandise is expended as largely in the burying of Christians as in the fumigating of the gods. At any rate, you say, the temple revenues are every day falling off: how few now throw in a contribution! In truth, we are not able to give alms both to your human and your heavenly mendicants; nor do we think that we are required to give any but to those who ask for it. Let Jupiter then hold out his hand and get, for our compassion spends more in the streets than yours does in the temples. But your other taxes will acknowledge a debt of gratitude to Christians; for in the faithfulness which keeps us from fraud upon a brother, we make conscience of paying all their dues: so that, by ascertaining how much is lost by fraud and falsehood in the census declarations—the calculation may easily be made—it would be seen that the ground of complaint in one department of revenue is compensated by the advantage which others derive.

Chapter XLIII.

I will confess, however, without hesitation, that there are some who in a sense may complain of Christians that they are a sterile race: as, for instance, pimps, and panders, and bath-suppliers; assassins, and poisoners, and sorcerers; soothsayers, too, diviners, and astrologers. But it is a noble fruit of Christians, that they have no fruits for such as these. And yet, whatever loss your interests suffer from the religion we profess, the protection you have from us makes amply up for it. What value do you set on persons, I do not here urge who deliver you from demons, I do not urge who for your sakes present prayers before the throne of the true God, for perhaps you have no belief in that—but from whom you can have nothing to fear?

Chapter XLIV.

Yes, and no one considers what the loss is to the common weal,—a loss as great as it is real, no one estimates the injury entailed upon the state, when, men of virtue as we are, we are put to death in such numbers; when so many of the truly good suffer the last penalty. And here we call your own acts to witness, you who are daily presiding at the trials of prisoners, and passing sentence upon crimes. Well, in your long lists of those accused of many and various atrocities, has any assassin, any cutpurse, any man guilty of sacrilege, or seduction, or stealing bathers' clothes, his name entered as being a Christian too? Or when Christians are brought before you on the mere ground of their name, is there ever found among them an ill-doer of the sort? It is always with your folk the prison is steaming, the mines are sighing, the wild beasts are fed: it is from you the exhibitors of gladiatorial shows always get their herds of criminals to feed up for the occasion. You find no Christian there, except simply as being such; or if one is there as something else, a Christian he is no longer.

Chapter XLV.

We, then, alone are without crime. Is there ought wonderful in that, if it be a very necessity with us? For a necessity indeed it is. Taught of God himself what goodness is, we have both a perfect knowledge of it as revealed to us by a perfect Master; and faithfully we do His will, as enjoined on us by a Judge we dare not despise. But your ideas of virtue you have got from mere human opinion; on human authority, too, its obligation rests: hence your system of practical morality is deficient, both in the fullness and authority requisite to produce a life of real virtue. Man's wisdom to point out what is good, is no greater than his authority to exact the keeping of it; the one is as easily deceived as the other is despised. And so, which is the ampler rule, to say, "Thou shalt not kill," or to teach, "Be not even angry?" Which is more perfect, to forbid adultery, or to restrain from even a single lustful look? Which indicates the higher intelligence, interdicting evil-doing, or evil-speaking? Which is more thorough, not allowing an injury, or not even suffering an injury done to you to be repaid? Though withal you know that these very laws also of yours, which seem to lead to virtue, have been borrowed from the law of God as the ancient model. Of the age of Moses we have already spoken. But what is the real authority of human laws, when it is in man's power both to evade them, by generally managing to hide himself out of sight in his crimes, and to despise them sometimes, if inclination or necessity leads him to offend? Think of these things, too, in the light of the brevity of any punishment you can inflict—never to last longer than till death. On this ground Epicurus makes light of all suffering and pain, maintaining that if it is small, it is contemptible; and if it is great, it is not long-continued. No doubt about it, we, who receive our awards under the judgment of an all-seeing God, and who look forward to eternal punishment from Him for sin,—we alone make real effort to attain a blameless life, under the influence of our ampler knowledge, the impossibility of concealment, and the greatness of the threatened torment, not merely long-enduring but everlasting, fearing Him, whom he too should fear who the fearing judges,—even God, I mean, and not the proconsul.

Chapter XLVI.

We have sufficiently met, as I think, the accusation of the various crimes on the ground of which these fierce demands are made for Christian blood. We have made a full exhibition of our case; and we have shown you how we are able to prove that our statement is correct, from the trustworthiness, I mean, and antiquity of our sacred writings, and from the confession likewise of the powers of spiritual wickedness themselves. Who will venture to undertake our refutation; not with skill of words, but, as we have managed our demonstration, on the basis of reality? But while the truth we hold is made clear to all, unbelief meanwhile, at the very time it is convinced of the worth of Christianity, which has now become well known for its benefits as well as from the intercourse of life, takes up the notion that it is not really a thing divine, but rather a kind of philosophy. These are the very things, it says, the philosophers counsel and profess—innocence, justice, patience, sobriety, chastity. Why, then, are we not permitted an equal liberty and impunity for our doctrines as they have, with whom, in respect of what we teach, we are compared? or why are not they, as so like us, not pressed to the same offices, for declining which our lives are imperiled? For who compels a philosopher to sacrifice or take an oath, or put out useless lamps at midday? Nay, they openly overthrow your gods, and in their writings they attack your superstitions; and you applaud them for it. Many of them even, with your countenance, bark out against your rulers, and are rewarded with statues and salaries, instead of being given to the wild beasts. And very right it should be so. For they are called philosophers, not Christians. This name of philosopher has no power to put demons to the rout. Why are they not able to do that too? since philosophers count demons inferior to gods. Socrates used to say, "If the demon grant permission." Yet he, too, though in denying the existence of your divinities he had a glimpse of the truth, at his dying ordered a cock to be sacrificed to Æsculapius, I believe in honor of his father, for Apollo pronounced Socrates the wisest of men. Thoughtless Apollo! testifying to the wisdom of the man who denied the existence of his race. In proportion to the enmity the truth awakens, you give offence by faithfully standing by it; but the man who corrupts and makes a mere pretence of it precisely on this ground gains favor with its persecutors. The truth which philosophers, these mockers and corrupters of it, with hostile ends merely affect to hold, and in doing so deprave, caring for naught but glory, Christians both intensely and intimately long for and maintain in its integrity, as those who have a real concern about their salvation. So that we are like each other neither in our knowledge nor our ways, as you imagine. For what certain information did Thales, the first of natural philosophers, give in reply to the inquiry of Croesus regarding Deity, the delay for further thought so often proving in vain? There is not a Christian workman but finds out God, and manifests Him, and hence assigns to Him all those attributes which go to constitute a divine being, though Plato affirms that it is far from easy to discover the Maker of the universe; and when He is found, it is difficult to make Him known to all. But if we challenge you to comparison in the virtue of chastity, I turn to a part of the sentence passed by the Athenians against Socrates, who was pronounced a corrupter of youth. The Christian confines himself to the female sex. I have read also how the harlot Phryne kindled in Diogenes the fires of lust, and how a certain Speusippus, of Plato's school, perished in the adulterous act. The Christian husband has nothing to do with any but his own wife. Democritus, in putting out his eyes, because he could not look on women without lusting after them, and was pained if his passion was not satisfied, owns plainly, by the punishment he inflicts, his incontinence. But a Christian with grace-healed eyes is sightless in this matter; he is mentally blind against the assaults of passion. If I maintain our superior modesty of behavior, there at once occurs to me Diogenes with filth-covered feet trampling on the proud couches of Plato, under the influence of another pride: the Christian does not even play the proud man to the pauper. If sobriety of spirit be the virtue in debate, why, there are Pythagoras at Thurii, and Zeno at Priene, ambitious of the supreme power: the Christian does not aspire to the ædileship. If equanimity be the contention, you have Lycurgus choosing death by self-starvation, because the Lacons had made some emendation of his laws: the Christian, even when he is condemned, gives thanks. If the comparison be made in regard to trustworthiness, Anaxagoras denied the deposit of his enemies: the Christian is noted for his fidelity even among those who are not of his religion. If the matter of sincerity is to be brought to trial, Aristotle basely thrust his friend Hermias from his place: the Christian does no harm even to his foe. With equal baseness does Aristotle play the sycophant to Alexander, instead of exercising to keep him in the right way, and Plato allows himself to be bought by Dionysius for his belly's sake. Aristippus in the purple, with all his great show of gravity, gives way to extravagance; and Hippias is put to death laying plots against the state: no Christian ever attempted such a thing in behalf of his brethren, even when persecution was scattering them abroad with every atrocity. But it will be said that some of us, too, depart from the rules of our discipline. In that case, however, we count them no longer Christians; but the philosophers who do such things retain still the name and the honor of wisdom. So, then, where is there any likeness between the Christian and the philosopher? Between the disciple of Greece and of heaven? between the man whose object is fame, and whose object is life? between the talker and the doer? between the man who builds up and the man who pulls down? between the friend and the foe of error? between one who corrupts the truth, and one who restores and teaches it? between its chief and its custodier?

Chapter XLVII.

Unless I am utterly mistaken, there is nothing so old as the truth; and the already proved antiquity of the divine writings is so far of use to me, that it leads men more easily to take it in that they are the treasure-source whence all later wisdom has been taken. And were it not necessary to keep my work to a moderate size, I might launch forth also into the proof of this. What poet or sophist has not drunk at the fountain of the prophets? Thence, accordingly, the philosophers watered their arid minds, so that it is the things they have from us which bring us into comparison with them. For this reason, I imagine, philosophy was banished by certain states—I mean by the Thebans, by the Spartans also, and the Argives—its disciples sought to imitate our doctrines; and ambitious, as I have said, of glory and eloquence alone, if they fell upon anything in the collection of sacred Scriptures which displeased them, in their own peculiar style of research, they perverted it to serve their purpose: for they had no adequate faith in their divinity to keep them from changing them, nor had they any sufficient understanding of them, either, as being still at the time under veil—even obscure to the Jews themselves, whose peculiar possession they seemed to be. For so, too, if the truth was distinguished by its simplicity, the more on that account the fastidiousness of man, too proud to believe, set to altering it; so that even what they found certain they made uncertain by their admixtures. Finding a simple revelation of God, they proceeded to dispute about Him, not as He had revealed to them, but turned aside to debate about His properties, His nature, His abode. Some assert Him to be incorporeal; others maintain He has a body,—the Platonists teaching the one doctrine, and the Stoics the other. Some think that He is composed of atoms, others of numbers: such are the different views of Epicurus and Pythagoras. One thinks He is made of fire; so it appeared to Heraclitus. The Platonists, again, hold that He administers the affairs of the world; the Epicureans, on the contrary, that He is idle and inactive, and, so to speak, a nobody in human things. Then the Stoics represent Him as placed outside the world, and whirling round this huge mass from without like a potter; while the Platonists place Him within the world, as a pilot is in the ship he steers. So, in like manner, they differ in their views about the world itself, whether it is created or uncreated, whether it is destined to pass away or to remain forever. So again it is debated concerning the nature of the soul, which some contend is divine and eternal, while others hold that it is dissoluble. According to each one's fancy, He has introduced either something new, or refashioned the old. Nor need we wonder if the speculations of philosophers have perverted the older Scriptures. Some of their brood, with their opinions, have even adulterated our new-given Christian revelation, and corrupted it into a system of philosophic doctrines, and from the one path have struck off many and inexplicable by-roads. And I have alluded to this, lest anyone becoming acquainted with the variety of parties among us, this might seem to him to put us on a level with the philosophers, and he might condemn the truth from the different ways in which it is defended. But we at once put in a plea in bar against these tainters of our purity, asserting that this is the rule of truth which comes down from Christ by transmission through His companions, to whom we shall prove that those devisers of different doctrines are all posterior. Everything opposed to the truth has been got up from the truth itself, the spirits of error carrying on this system of opposition. By them all corruptions of wholesome discipline have been secretly instigated; by them, too, certain fables have been introduced, that, by their resemblance to the truth, they might impair its credibility, or vindicate their own higher claims to faith; so that people might think Christians unworthy of credit because the poets or philosophers are so, or might regard the poets and philosophers as worthier of confidence from their not being followers of Christ. Accordingly, we get ourselves laughed at for proclaiming that God will one day judge the world. For, like us, the poets and philosophers set up a judgment-seat in the realms below. And if we threaten Gehenna, which is a reservoir of secret fire under the earth for purposes of punishment, we have in the same way derision heaped on us. For so, too, they have their Pyriphlegethon, a river of flame in the regions of the dead. And if we speak of Paradise, the place of heavenly bliss appointed to receive the spirits of the saints, severed from the knowledge of this world by that fiery zone as by a sort of enclosure, the Elysian plains have taken possession of their faith. Whence is it, I pray you have all this, so like us, in the poets and philosophers? The reason simply is, that they have been taken from our religion. But if they are taken from our sacred things, as being of earlier date, then ours are the truer, and have higher claims upon belief, since even their imitations find faith among you. If they maintain their sacred mysteries to have sprung from their own minds, in that case ours will be reflections of what are later than themselves, which by the nature of things is impossible, for never does the shadow precede the body which casts it, or the image the reality.

Chapter XLVIII.

Come now, if some philosopher affirms, as Laberius holds, following an opinion of Pythagoras, that a man may have his origin from a mule, a serpent from a woman, and with skill of speech twists every argument to prove his view, will he not gain acceptance for and work in some the conviction that, on account of this, they should even abstain from eating animal food? May anyone have the persuasion that he should so abstain, lest by chance in his beef he eats of some ancestor of his? But if a Christian promises the return of a man from a man, and the very actual Gaius from Gaius, the cry of the people will be to have him stoned; they will not even so much as grant him a hearing. If there is any ground for the moving to and fro of human souls into different bodies, why may they not return into the very substance they have left, seeing this is to be restored, to be that which had been? They are no longer the very things they had been; for they could not be what they were not, without first ceasing to be what they had been. If we were inclined to give all rein upon this point, discussing into what various beasts one and another might probably be changed, we would need at our leisure to take up many points. But this we would do chiefly in our own defense, as setting forth what is greatly worthier of belief, that a man will come back from a man—any given person from any given person, still retaining his humanity; so that the soul, with its qualities unchanged, may be restored to the same condition, thought not to the same outward framework. Assuredly, as the reason why restoration takes place at all is the appointed judgment, every man must needs come forth the very same who had once existed, that he may receive at God's hands a judgment, whether of good desert or the opposite. And therefore the body too will appear; for the soul is not capable of suffering without the solid substance (that is, the flesh; and for this reason, also) that it is not right that souls should have all the wrath of God to bear: they did not sin without the body, within which all was done by them. But how, you say, can a substance which has been dissolved be made to reappear again? Consider thyself, O man, and thou wilt believe in it! Reflect on what you were before you came into existence. Nothing. For if you had been anything, you would have remembered it. You, then, who were nothing before you existed, reduced to nothing also when you cease to be, why may you not come into being again out of nothing, at the will of the same Creator whose will created you out of nothing at the first? Will it be anything new in your case? You who were not, *were* made; when you cease to be again, you *shall* be made. Explain, if you can, your original creation, and then demand to know how you shall be re-created. Indeed, it will be still easier surely to make you what you were once, when the very same creative power made you without difficulty what you never were before. There will be doubts, perhaps, as to the power of God, of Him who hung in its place this huge body of our world, made out of what had never existed, as from a death of emptiness and inanity, animated by the Spirit who quickens all living things, its very self the unmistakable type of the resurrection, that it might be to you a witness—nay, the exact image of the resurrection. Light, every day extinguished, shines out again; and, with like alternation, darkness succeeds light's outgoing. The defunct stars re-live; the seasons, as soon as they are finished, renew their course; the fruits are brought to maturity, and then are reproduced. The seeds do not spring up with abundant produce, save as they rot and dissolve away;— all things are preserved by perishing, all things are refashioned out of death. Thou, man of nature so exalted, if thou understandest thyself, taught even by the Pythian words, lord of all these things that die and rise,—shalt thou die to perish evermore? Wherever your dissolution shall have taken place, whatever material agent has destroyed you, or swallowed you up, or swept you away, or reduced you to nothingness, it shall again restore you. Even nothingness is His who is Lord of *all*.

You ask, Shall we then be always dying, and rising up from death? If so the Lord of all things had appointed, you would have to submit, though unwillingly, to the law of your creation. But, in fact, He has no other purpose than that of which He has informed us. The Reason which made the universe out of diverse elements, so that all things might be composed of opposite substances in unity—of void and solid, of animate and inanimate, of comprehensible and incomprehensible, of light and darkness, of life itself and death—has also disposed time into order, by fixing and distinguishing its mode, according to which this first portion of it, which we inhabit from the beginning of the world, flows down by a temporal course to a close; but the portion which succeeds, and to which we look forward continues forever. When, therefore, the boundary and limit, that millennial interspace, has been passed, when even the outward fashion of the world itself—which has been spread like a veil over the eternal economy, equally a thing of time—passes away, then the whole human race shall be raised again, to have its dues meted out according as it has merited in the period of good or evil, and thereafter to have these paid out through the immeasurable ages of eternity. Therefore after this there is neither death nor repeated resurrections, but we shall be the same that we are now, and still unchanged—the servants of God, ever with God, clothed upon with the proper substance of eternity; but the profane, and all who are not true worshippers of God, in like manner shall be consigned to the punishment of everlasting fire—that fire which, from its very nature indeed, directly ministers to their incorruptibility. The philosophers are familiar as well as we with the distinction between a common and a secret fire. Thus that which is in common use is far different from that which we see in divine judgments, whether striking as thunderbolts from heaven, or bursting up out of the earth through mountain-tops; for it does not consume what it scorches, but while it burns it repairs. So the mountains continue ever burning; and a person struck by lighting is even now kept safe from any destroying flame. A notable proof this

The Apology

of the fire eternal! A notable example of the endless judgment which still supplies punishment with fuel! The mountains burn, and last. How will it be with the wicked and the enemies of God?

Chapter XLIX.

These are what are called presumptuous speculations in our case alone; in the philosophers and poets they are regarded as sublime speculations and illustrious discoveries. They are men of wisdom, we are fools. They are worthy of all honor, we are folk to have the finger pointed at; nay, besides that, we are even to have punishments inflicted on us. But let things which are the defense of virtue, if you will, have no foundation, and give them duly the name of fancies, yet still they are necessary; let them be absurd if you will, yet they are of use: they make all who believe them better men and women, under the fear of never-ending punishment and the hope of never-ending bliss. It is not, then, wise to brand as false, nor to regard as absurd, things the truth of which it is expedient to presume. On no ground is it right positively to condemn as bad what beyond all doubt is profitable. Thus, in fact, you are guilty of the very presumption of which you accuse us, in condemning what is useful. It is equally out of the question to regard them as nonsensical; at any rate, if they are false and foolish, they hurt nobody. For they are just (in that case) like many other things on which you inflict no penalties—foolish and fabulous things, I mean, which, as quite innocuous, are never charged as crimes or punished. But in a thing of the kind, if this be so indeed, we should be adjudged to ridicule, not to swords, and flames, and crosses, and wild beasts, in which iniquitous cruelty not only the blinded populace exults and insults over us, but in which some of you too glory, not scrupling to gain the popular favor by your injustice. As though all you can do to us did not depend upon our pleasure. It is assuredly a matter of my own inclination, being a Christian. Your condemnation, then, will only reach me in that case, if I wish to be condemned; but when all you can do to me, you can do only at my will, all you can do is dependent on my will, and is not in your power. The joy of the people in our trouble is therefore utterly reasonless. For it is our joy they appropriate to themselves, since we would far rather be condemned than apostatize from God; on the contrary, our haters should be sorry rather than rejoice, as we have obtained the very thing of our own choice.

Chapter L.

In that case, you say, why do you complain of our persecutions? You ought rather to be grateful to us for giving you the sufferings you want. Well, it is quite true that it is our desire to suffer, but it is in the way that the soldier longs for war. No one indeed suffers willingly, since suffering necessarily implies fear and danger. Yet the man who objected to the conflict, both fights with all his strength, and when victorious, he rejoices in the battle, because he reaps from it glory and spoil. It is our battle to be summoned to your tribunals that there, under fear of execution, we may battle for the truth. But the day is won when the object of the struggle is gained. This victory of ours gives us the glory of pleasing God, and the spoil of life eternal. But we are overcome. Yes, when we have obtained our wishes. Therefore we conquer in dying; we go forth victorious at the very time we are subdued. Call us, if you like, *Sarmenticii* and *Semaxii*, because, bound to a half-axle stake, we are burned in a circle-heap of fagots. This is the attitude in which we conquer, it is our victoryrobe, it is for us a sort of triumphal car. Naturally enough, therefore, we do not please the vanquished; on account of this, indeed, we are counted a desperate, reckless race. But the very desperation and recklessness you object to in us, among yourselves lift high the standard of virtue in the cause of glory and of fame. Mucius of his own will left his right hand on the altar: what sublimity of mind! Empedocles gave his whole body at Catana to the fires of Ætna: what mental resolution! A certain foundress of Carthage gave herself away in second marriage to the funeral pile: what a noble witness of her chastity! Regulus, not wishing that his one life should count for the lives of many enemies, endured these crosses over all his frame: how brave a man—even in captivity a conqueror! Anaxarchus, when he was being beaten to death by a barley-pounder, cried out, "Beat on, beat on at the case of Anaxarchus; no stroke falls on Anaxarchus himself." O magnanimity of the philosopher, who even in such an end had jokes upon his lips! I omit all reference to those who with their own sword, or with any other milder form of death, have bargained for glory. Nay, see how even torture contests are crowned by you. The Athenian courtezan, having wearied out the executioner, at last bit off her tongue and spat it in the face of the raging tyrant, that she might at the same time spit away her power of speech, nor be longer able to confess her fellow-conspirators, if even overcome, that might be her inclination. Zeno the Eleatic, when he was asked by Dionysius what good philosophy did, on answering that it gave contempt of death, was all unquailing, given over to the tyrant's scourge, and sealed his opinion even to the death. We all know how the Spartan lash, applied with the utmost cruelty under the very eyes of friends encouraging, confers on those who bear it honor proportionate to the blood which the young men shed. O glory legitimate, because it is human, for whose sake it is counted neither reckless foolhardiness, nor desperate obstinacy, to despise death itself and all sorts of savage treatment; for whose sake you may for your native place, for the empire, for friendship, endure all you are forbidden to do for God! And you cast statues in honor of persons such as these, and you put inscriptions upon images, and cut out epitaphs on tombs, that their names may never perish. In so far you can by your monuments, you yourselves afford a sort of resurrection to the dead. Yet he who expects the true resurrection from God, is insane, if for God he suffers! But go zealously on, good presidents, you will stand higher with the people if you sacrifice the Christians at their wish, kill us, torture us, condemn us, grind us to dust; your injustice is the proof that we are innocent. Therefore God suffers that we thus suffer; for but very lately, in condemning a Christian woman to the *leno* rather than to the *leo* you made confession that a taint on our purity is considered among us something more terrible than any punishment and any death. Nor does your cruelty, however exquisite, avail you; it is rather a temptation to us. The oftener we are mown down by you, the more in number we grow; *the blood of Christians is seed*. Many of your writers exhort to the courageous bearing of pain and death, as Cicero in the *Tusculans*, as Seneca in his *Chances*, as Diogenes, Pyrrhus, Callinicus; and yet their words do not find so many disciples as Christians do, teachers not by words, but by their deeds. That very obstinacy you rail against is the preceptress. For who that contemplates it, is not excited to inquire what is at the bottom of it? who, after inquiry, does not embrace our doctrines? and when he has embraced them, desires not to suffer that he may become partaker of the fullness of God's grace, that he may obtain from God complete forgiveness, by giving in exchange his blood? For that secures the remission of all offences. On this account it is that we return thanks on the very spot for your sentences. As the divine and human are ever opposed to each other, when we are condemned by you, we are acquitted by the Highest.

Elucidations.

I.

(Arrangement, p. 4, *supra.*)

The arrangement I have adopted in editing these Edinburgh Translations of Tertullian is a practical one. It will be found logical and helpful to the student, who is referred to the Prefatory pages of this volume for an Elucidation of the difficulties, with which any arrangement of these treatises is encumbered. For, *first*, an attempt to place them in chronological order is out of the question; and, *second*, all efforts to separate precisely the Orthodox from the Montanistic or Montanist works of our author have hitherto defied the acumen of critics. It would be mere empiricism for me to attempt an original classification in the face of questions which even experts have been unable to determine.

If we bear in mind, however, a few guiding facts, we shall see that difficulties are less than might appear, assuming our object to be a practical one. (1.) Only *four* of these essays were written against Orthodoxy; (2.) *five* more are reckoned as wholly uncertain, which amounts to saying that they are not positively heretical. (3.) Again, *five* are colorless, as to Montanism, and hence should be reputed Orthodox. (4.) Of others, written after the influences of Montanism had, more or less, tainted his doctrine, the whole are yet valuable and some are noble defenses of the Catholic Faith. (5.) Finally eight or ten of his treatises were written while he was a Catholic, and are precious contributions to the testimony of the Primitive Church.

From these facts, we may readily conclude that the mass of Tertullian's writings is Orthodox. Some of them are to be read with caution; others, again, must be rejected for their heresy; but yet all are most instructive historically, and as defining even by errors "the faith once delivered to the Saints." I propose to note those which require caution as we pass them in review. Those written against the Church are classed by themselves, at the end of the list, and all the rest may be read with confidence. A most interesting inquiry arises in connection with the quotations from Scripture to be found in our author. Did a Latin version exist in his day, or does he translate from the Greek of the New Testament and the LXX? A paradoxical writer (Semler) contends that Tertullian "never used a Greek ms." (see Kaye, p. 106.) But Tertullian's rugged

Latin betrays everywhere his familiarity with Greek idioms and forms of thought. He wrote, also, in Greek, and there is no reason to doubt that he knew the Greek Scriptures primarily, if he knew any Greek whatever. Possibly we owe to Tertullian the *primordia* of the Old African Latin Versions, some of which seem to have contained the disputed text 1 John v. 7; of which more when we come to the Praxeas. For the present in the absence of definite evidence we must infer that Tertullian usually translated from the LXX, and from the originals of the New Testament. But Mosheim thinks the progress of the Gospel in the West was now facilitated by the existence of Latin Versions. Observe, also, Kaye's important note, p. 293, and his reference to Lardner, *Cred.* xxvii. 19.

II.

(Address to Magistrates, cap. i., p. 17.)

The Apology comes first in order, on logical grounds. It is classed with our author's orthodox works by Neander, and pronounced colorless by Kaye. It is the noblest of his productions in its purpose and spirit, and it falls in with the Primitive System of Apologetics. I have placed next in order to it several treatises, mostly unblemished, which are of the same character; which defend the cause of Christians against Paganism, against Gentile Philosophy, and against Judaism; closing this portion by the two books *Ad Nationes*, which may be regarded as a recapitulation of the author's arguments, especially those to be found in the Apology. In these successive works, as compared with those of Justin Martyr, we obtain a fair view of the progressive relations of the Church with the Roman Empire and with divers antagonistic systems in the East and West.

III.

(History of Christians, cap. ii., p. 18.)

The following Chronological outline borrowed from the Benedictines and from Bishop Kaye, will prove serviceable here.

Tertullian born (*circa*) a.d. 150.
Tertullian converted (*surmise*) 185.
Tertullian married (*say*) 186.
Tertullian ordained presbyter (*circa*) 192.
Tertullian lapsed (*circa*) 200.
Tertullian deceased (extreme surmise) 240.

The Imperial history of his period may be thus arranged:

Birth of Caracalla a.d. 188.
Birth of Geta 189.
Reign of Severus 193.
Defeat of Niger 195.
Caracalla made a *Cæsar* 196.
Capture of Byzantium 196.
Defeat of Albinus 197.
Geta made a *Cæsar* 198.
Caracalla called *Augustus* 198.
Caracalla associated in the Empire 198.
War against the Parthians 198.
Severus returns from the war 203.
Celebration of the Secular Games 204.
Plautianus put to death (*circa*) 205.
Geta called *Augustus* 208.
War in Britain 208.
Wall of Severus 210.
Death of Severus 211.

IV.

(Tiberius, capp. v. and xxiv., pp. 22 and 35.)

A fair examination of what has been said on this subject, *pro* and *con*, may be found in Kaye's *Tertullian*, pp. 102–105. In his abundant candor this author leans to the doubters, but in stating the case he seems to me to fortify the position of Lardner and Mosheim. What the brutal Tiberius may have thought or done with respect to Pilate's report concerning the holy victim of his judicial injustice is of little importance to the believer. Nevertheless, as matter of history it deserves attention. Great stress is to be placed on the fact that Tertullian was probably a jurisconsult, familiar with the Roman archives, and influenced by them in his own acceptance of Divine Truth. It is not supposable that such a man would have hazarded his bold appeal to the records, in remonstrating with the Senate and in the very faces of the Emperor and his colleagues, had he not known that the evidence was irrefragable.

V.

(The darkness at the Crucifixion, cap. xxi., p. 35.)

Kaye disappoints us (p. 150) in his slight notice of this most interesting subject. Without attempting to discuss the story of Phlegon and other points which afford Gibbon an opportunity for misplaced sneering, such as even a Pilate would have rebuked, while it may be well to recall the exposition of Milman, at the close of Gibbon's fifteenth chapter, I must express my own preference for another view. This will be found candidly summed up and stated, in the Speaker's Commentary, in the concise note on St. Matt. xxvii. 45.

VI.

(Numbers of the Faithful, cap. xxxvii., p. 45.)

Kaye, as usual, gives this vexed question a candid survey. Making all allowances, however, I accept the conjecture of some reputable authorities, that there were 2,000,000 of Christians, in the bounds of the Roman Empire at the close of the Second Century. So mightily grew the testimony of Jesus and prevailed. When we reflect that only a century intervened between the times of Tertullian and the conversion of the Roman Emperor, it is not easy to regard our author's language as merely that of fervid genius and of rhetorical hyperbole. He could not have ventured upon exaggeration without courting scorn as well as defeat. What he affirms is probable in the nature of the case. Were it otherwise, then the conditions, which, in a single century rendered it possible for Constantine to effect the greatest revolution in mind and manners that has ever been known among men, would be a miracle compared with which that of his alleged Vision of the Cross sinks into insignificance. To this subject it will be necessary to recur hereafter.

VII.

(Christian usages, cap. xxxix., p. 46.)

A candid review of the matters discussed in this chapter will be found in Kaye (pp. 146, 209.) The important fact is there clearly stated that "the primitive Christians scrupulously complied with the decree pronounced by the Apostles at Jerusalem in abstaining from things strangled and from blood" (Acts xv. 20). On this subject consult the references given in the Speaker's Commentary, *ad locum*. The

Greeks, to their honour, still maintain this prohibition, but St. Augustine's great authority relaxed the Western scruples on this matter, for he regarded it as a decree of temporary obligation, while the Hebrew and Gentile Christians were in peril of misunderstanding and estrangement.

On the important question as to the cessation of miracles Kaye takes a somewhat original position. But see his interesting discussion and that of the late Professor Hey, in Kaye's *Tertullian*, pp. 80–102, 151–161. I do not think writers on these subjects have sufficiently distinguished between *miracles* properly so called, and *providences* vouchsafed in answer to prayer. There was no *miracle* in the case of the Thundering Legion, assuming the story to be true; and I dare to affirm that marked answers to prayer, by *providential interpositions*, but wholly distinct from miraculous agencies, have never ceased among those who "ask in the Son's Name." Such interpositions are often *preternatural* only; that is, they economize certain powers which, though natural in themselves, lie outside of the System of Nature with which we happen to be familiar. This distinction has been overlooked.

VIII.

(Multitudes, cap. xl., p. 47.)

Note the words—"*multitudes* to a single beast." Can it be possible that Tertullian would use such language to the magistrates, if he knew that such sentences were of rare occurrence? The disposition of our times to *minimize* the persecutions of our Christian forefathers calls upon us to note such references, all the more important because occurring *obiter* and mentioned as notorious. Note also, the closing chapter of this Apology, and reference to the outcries of the populace, in Cap. xxxv. See admirable remarks on the benefits derived by the Church from the sufferings of Christian martyrs, with direct reference to Tertullian, Wordsworth, *Church Hist. to Council of Nicæa*, cap. xxiv., p. 374.

IX.

(Christian manners, cap. xlii., p. 49.)

      A study of the manners of Christians, in the Ante-Nicene Age, as sketched by the unsparing hand of Tertullian, will convince any unprejudiced mind of the mighty power of the Holy Ghost, in framing such characters out of heathen originals. When, under Montanistic influences our severely ascetic author complains of the Church's corruptions, and turns inside-out the whole estate of the faithful, we see all that can be pressed on the other side; but, this very important chapter must be borne in mind, together with the closing sentence of chap. xliv., as evidence that whatever might be said by a rigid disciplinarian, the Church, *as compared with* our day, was still a living embodiment of Philippians iv. 8.

X.

(Paradise, cap. xlvii., p. 52.)

      See Kaye, p. 248. Our author seems not always consistent with himself in his references to the Places of departed spirits. Kaye thinks he identifies Paradise with the Heaven of the Most High, in one place (the *De Exhort. Cast.*, xiii.) where he probably confuses the Apostle's ideas, in Galatians v. 12, and Ephesians v. 5. *Commonly*, however, though he is not consistent with himself, this would be his scheme:—
      1. The *Inferi*, or *Hades*, where the soul of Dives was in one continent and that of Lazarus in another, with a gulf between. Our author places "Abraham's bosom" in Hades.

2. *Paradise*. In Hades, but in a superior and more glorious region. This more blessed abode was opened to the souls of the martyrs and other greater saints, at our Lord's descent into the place of the dead. After the General Resurrection and Judgment, there remain:

1. *Gehenna*, for the lost, prepared for the devil and his angels.

2. The *Heaven of Heavens*, the eternal abode of the righteous, in the vision of the Lord and His Eternal Joy.

Tertullian's variations on this subject will force us to recur to it hereafter; but, here it may be noted that the confusions of Latin Christianity received their character in this particular, from the genius of our author. Augustine caught from him a certain indecision about the terms and places connected with the state of the departed which has continued, to this day, to perplex theologians in the West. Taking advantage of such confusions, the stupendous Roman system of "Purgatory" was fabricated in the middle ages; but the Greeks never accepted it, and it differs fundamentally from what the earlier Latin Fathers, including Tertullian, have given us as speculations.

XI.

(The Leo and the Leno, cap. l., p. 55.)

Here we find the alliterative and epigrammatic genius of Tertullian anticipating a similar poetic charm in Augustine. The Christian maid or matron preferred the *Leo* to the *leno*; to be devoured rather than to be debauched. Our author wrests a tribute to the chastity of Christian women from the cruelty of their judges, who recognizing this fact, were accustomed as a refinement of their injustice to give sentence against them, refusing the mercy of a horrible death, by committing them to the ravisher: "damnando Christianam *ad lenonem* potius quam *ad leonem*."

XII.

(The Seed of the Church, cap. l., p. 55.)

Kaye has devoted a number of his pages to the elucidation of this subject, not only showing the constancy of the martyrs, but illustrating the fact that Christians, like St. Paul, were forced to "die daily," even when they were not subjected to the fiery trial. He who confessed himself a Christian made himself a social outcast. All manner of outrages and wrongs could be committed against him with impunity. Rich men, who had joined themselves to Christ, were forced to accept "the spoiling of their goods." Brothers denounced brothers, and husbands their wives; "a man's foes were they of his own household." But the Church triumphed through suffering, and "out of weakness was made strong."

Made in the USA
Monee, IL
23 February 2023

28520650R00075